Explaining Judaism to Jews and Christians

By Rabbi Samuel M. Silver

Artwork by Norman Manaly

New York

This book is dedicated to our five sons—
Leon, Joshua, Barry, Noah and Daniel

296
SIL

Published by Arco Publishing Company, Inc.
219 Park Avenue South, New York, N.Y. 10003

Library of Congress Catalog Card Number 72-96799

ISBN   0-668-02958-7 (Library Edition)
ISBN   0-668-02943-9 (Paper Edition)

Printed in the United States of America

Table of Contents

שְׁמַע יִשְׂרָאֵל יְהֹוָה אֱלֹהֵינוּ יְהֹוָה ׀ אֶחָד׃

"Shema Yisroel Adonoi Elohenu Adonoi Echod"

Hear, O Israel,
the Lord our God,
the Lord is One

Judaism—
Some of Its Chief Emphases

Judaism is a faith which likes to explain itself. The spokesmen of Judaism have always hearkened |to the precept laid down by the prophet (Isaiah) who said (Chap. 1, verse 18), "Come, let us reason together." Jews are willing to accept the challenge that a Jewish belief which cannot be buttressed by logic need not be accepted. We prefer not to ask our people to accept a doctrine "on faith alone."

Of course, there are certain contentions which simply cannot be verified as one does in laboratory style. But even beliefs which defy actual demonstration must stand the test of reason. Such a belief, for example, is the fundamental one in the existence of God. We cannot show the skeptic the figure of God. We cannot prove beyond any doubt that there is a God. But we can adduce logical arguments to substantiate the belief. We can see, for example, that nothing in the world exists without reflecting a creator, a design, and a purpose. Shall we say, then that the only thing in the world which has no author is the world itself? It is a reasonable hypothesis to maintain that the universe, its symmetries and its systems, its intricacies and its complexities, reveal an order and therefore an author. It is also reasonable to believe that the existence of that ethical seismographic apparatus called the conscience, and the remarkable intimations and frequent efflorescense of nobility exhibited by human beings, indicate the divine implantation of good qualities, a theory beautifully dramatized by the Biblical story of Creation and the fashioning of man after God's pattern.

Hence, a good rational "case" for the existence of God can be made and has been made in Jewish writings. It is a hypothesis, perhaps, such as is often the basis of laboratory probing, but it is a "working" hypothesis.

Indeed, Judaism has been described as a program of righteous living for those who wish to live "as though" there were a God. In other words, Judaism recommends to its practitioners a behavior agenda which will strengthen the conviction among all men that the most desirable standard of conduct is a moral one. It is for these reasons that the prophets refer to the Jewish people as divine servants entrusted with a special mission to bear witness to the satisfaction which comes to men through the exercise of forbearance, compassion, study, mercy and justice.

The main emphasis in Judaism is upon the **absolute oneness of God** and the consequent unity of all His creatures. Properly absorbed, this understanding make violence, strife, and hatred not only undesirable but sacrilegious.

In some faiths it is believed that the farther one withdraws from society the holier one can be. In Judaism, on the contrary, it is believed that **holiness** can be established by immersing oneself into the affairs of men. One displays one's piety by the manner in which one conducts one's business, deals with one's neighbors and uses one's material resources; not by isolation or voluntary penury.

In Judaism we believe that man cannot expect totally to rely on God for the improvement of life. In our faith we see a relationship between God and man within the framework of the regulations which, in His grace, God has ordained for this world. The relationship is a kind of **partnership.** God inspires us and instills wisdom in us to understand the value and validity of the ethical way. Man must cooperate with God in the translation of worthy concepts into actual deeds. God, like a parent, in the Jewish view, will not coerce His children to do good. Man must cooperate.

This brings us to another aspect of the Jewish outlook. That is the conviction that **man's will is free.** We Jews do not believe that human fate is predestined or that certain eventualities are inevitable. Through the exercise of his will, man has the power to avert disasters, ameliorate worldly conditions and alter destiny. Because man's will is free he has the power to inflict hurt on others. For this reason, the innocent may become the victims of the waywardness and the cruelty of the uninhibited and the undisciplined.

There is a belief in **collective morality** in Judaism by which the group is held responsible for the education of the individual and the maximization of that restraint and solicitude for others which will lessen misery and increase well-being. Indeed, the stress on the solicitude for others is so powerful that in the Bible we are told that a man is obligated to give a portion of his worldly goods to the world's oppressed and under-privileged: the widow, the orphan, the destitute. **Charity** is almost compulsory and, in the view of one post-Biblical philosopher, the highest form of help is the kind which will enable the poor man to become free of the need for help.

Judaism does not believe that religion is a static thing. Indeed, the Bible contains evidence of the Jewish notion that man is engaged in discovering clearer and clearer views of God. One can see in Scriptures the **growth of the God-idea** from the fancy that He is a magician to the awesome intimation that He is the spirit which links man to man and man to the Universe. One cannot be regarded as thoroughly Jewish unless one

7

recognizes the limitations of one's present understanding and devotes oneself to never-ceasing study towards a better comprehension of God's expectations and their implementation on earth. The highest accolade in Jewish life goes to the scholar. Saints are unknown in Judaism but one may strive for saintliness with the cultural equipment which insight and learning provide. Just as Judaism is reluctant to believe that anyone can achieve unblemished sainthood, so it is equally loath to accept the idea that unrelieved villainy is possible. We reject the notion that man is innately evil because of the manner of his birth.. **Life is essentially good** and man is an arena of good and wicked impulses, with the former standing a fine chance of prevailing over the latter if enough effort is applied. We do not believe that any formula can wash away sin. Sin itself is regarded as a falling away from the mark. We overcome surrender to wickedness not by a prayer alone, though a prayer helps to fortify us for the struggle; not by a ceremony alone, though every ceremony is a memorandum of some significant principle; not by a confession alone, though a confession is a wholesome prod to repentance; not by a festival celebration alone, though a celebration tangibilizes some abstract virtue; but by actual deeds of goodness which lead to redemption and enduring regeneration.

The so-called **"chosen people"** concept in Judaism does not imply a belief that Jews are superior to others. As developed by the prophets, the idea is that since the Jews were the first to catch a glimpse of the unity in the world under a Creator who wants man to work towards goodness it is incumbent upon Jews to "bear witness" to this notion as widely as possible. This does not call for proselytism, although newcomers are welcomed into the fold, and many do opt to become Jews. But Jews do not conduct a missionary program to persuade others to become Jews; they are called upon to act in such a way as to turn people towards an acceptance of an ethical God. Jews, therefore, do not regard themselves as better in any way because of their blood or breeding. The Jews are not a race; they are a group of people held together by certain common beliefs and a common background. Often divided politically, they feel the same kinship towards one another as do families separated by national borders. The Jews feel that they do have a special assignment, not to dominate others, but to serve others; not to rule over others, but to be of aid to others; not to lord it over others, but to be the agents of mankind in their search for brotherhood and peace.

In Judaism, relatively minor stress is laid upon the world after this one, on **life after death,**etc. We do have confidence that the millions of years of human life and development cannot be wasted; that something as precious as the human spirit will not end in evaporation; that in some form or other, human personality will continue. But we do not predicate our entire faith and its observance upon the hope of qualifying for eternal bliss in another world. This is a mystery which is beyond our comprehension, one which can safely be left to God. If He had wanted us to know more about this matter He would have provided more information. Meanwhile, man has a life-time of good to do on this earth and the assignments in expanding the area of happiness in this world are compelling enough for the most compassionate and the most zealously pious.

Man can perhaps never become perfect, says Judaism, but he is blessed in that he is endowed by his Creator with the urge to brighten God's image through the excellence of his deeds and the hastening of an era when all of his fellow-creatures will know the taste of plenty, of equality, and of peace.

The huge candelabrum, with its seven holders, is a gift to the State of Israel from Great Britain. Situated in Jerusalem, it dramatizes the spiritual goals of the Jewish State. The Sabbath candelabrum reminds one that what one prays for on the Sabbath should be carried out during the other days of the week.

In the Synagogue

The Jewish house of worship is called either a synagogue, a temple, or a shul.

Temple is the term often reserved for the ancient sanctuary in Jerusalem. The Hebrew term is Beth Hamikdash (the House of Holiness). For that reason, those Jews who believe that God, in His own time, will restore the Jerusalem shrine and there re-activate the sacrificial system, do not refer to their places of prayer as temple.

Synagogue is a Greek word meaning "meeting place." Deprived of their sanctuary, the Jews in Babylonia (where they were taken captive after 586 B.C.E.-- before the Christian era) met for prayers in improvised places, which later came to be called synagogues.

The three functions of the synagogue are discerned in three Hebrew terms often used for it: (1) Beth Ha-Tefillah, house of prayer; (2) Beth Ha-Midrash, house of study; and (3) Beth Ha-Kneset, house of assembly or socialization.

The term, shul, is from the German, schule, school.

No two synagogues need look alike. But most of them do contain the following:

(1)   Pews, where the worshippers sit.

(2)   A pulpit, where the rabbi (a Hebrew word meaning teacher) officiates. Actually, a rabbi is not needed. Laymen may lead the service.

(3)   An Ark, a closet-like repository, called in Hebrew Aron Ha-Kodesh (Ark of Holiness), which contains the Torah Scrolls.

(4)   The Torah Scrolls. Torah is a Hebrew word meaning "teaching." It is also used to delineate the First Five Books of the Bible. It also refers to the Wooden Scroll around which the Five Books, written by hand on parchment, are wrapped.

(5)   The Eternal Light (Hebrew: Ner Tamid), a light over the Ark, symbolizing the continuity of divine providence.

(6)   The Star of David, Jewish insignia analagous to the Cross. As the Cross betokens something Christian, the Star of David (known in Hebrew as Shield of David, Mogen David), signifies something Jewish.

(7)   The Sabbath Candelabrum. Lights symbolizing the extra brightness which the Sabbath radiates.

(8)   Prayerbooks. One prayerbook containing liturgies for the Sabbath, weekdays and festivals is called Siddur (Procedure). The one for the High Holydays is called Machzor (Cycle).

Sabbath

The most important religious observance of the Jew is the Sabbath.

The word, Sabbath, is a Hebrew term that has entered the English language.

Sabbath means not only rest, cessation of work, but also uplift and re-creation. It is a time designed for relaxation, worship, study and the renewal of family fidelity.

When devised, the Sabbath was the greatest social advance of the epoch, for it put a stop to the limitless subjection of man by man.

Putting divine force behind a humanitarian measure, the architects of Judaism made it clear that the Lord Himself paused for a respite in His labor. If God rested, man should be permitted to rest.

Not only does the Bible open with the lesson that God Himself ordained a day of rest, but the Ten Commandments includes the decree that the Sabbath is mandated upon every human being.

There are actually two versions of the Ten Commandments in the Bible: Exodus 20 and Deuteronomy 5. The texts are substantially the same, but the rationale for the Sabbath differs in them. In Exodus we learn that the Seventh Day is a rest day because it was the Lord's rest day at the time of Creation. Hence, no one should toil then, not freemen, nor servants, nor even beasts of burden.

In the Deuteronomic text, the Sabbath is declared to be holy as a reminder that the Jews were themselves

The Hebrew word Shaddai means "Almighty One," and is seen in many synagogues, where the Torah Scroll is read, as pictured above.

victims of relentless taskmasters in Egypt until God delivered them. Jews were cautioned against being "Egyptianized."

The observance of the Sabbath, like that of all Jewish sacred seasons, begins at sunset.

The meal on Sabbath eve is festive. It is preceded by the blessings of the candles, symbols of light; and the wine, tokens of sweetness; and the bread, which is braided (termed challah) to indicate the extra measure of adornment which the Sabbath brings. Table songs and prayers are part of the home observance.

The wine blessing is called the Kiddush (sanctification) and its text refers to both historical bases for the Sabbath: the Creation and the Exodus.

The Sabbath is celebrated in the synagogue on Friday night and on Saturday. For many synagogues the Friday night service is the major gathering time for the congregation. The prayers, the songs, the sermon and the silent meditation are meant to attune the worshipper to the message of the Sabbath, that man can grow wiser, more reverent and gentler as well as older from week to week.

The Saturday morning worship service includes the reading from the Torah scroll. In some Reform temples, the Biblical reading from the parchment scroll also occurs on Friday night.

The traditionalist Jew abstains from toil on the Seventh Day. He will enjoy a snooze, a Sabbatical from his daily rounds, but also indulge in study both individually and in family groups, and in spiritual discussions.

The departure of the Sabbath is also the occasion for a religious exercise called Havdalah (Separation). The Sabbath, often referred to as a Queen, is escorted back into the work-a-day world.

In Hebrew Sabbath is pronounced Shabbos or Shabbat, and worshippers wish each other "Gut Shabbos," (Good Sabbath), or "Shabbat Shalom" (Sabbath of Peace).

Neither weddings nor funerals may take place on the Sabbath. Funerals are forbidden, for the day must be devoted to gladsome things. Weddings are not permitted because no other source of joy must "compete with Oneg Shabbat, "The Delight of the Sabbath."

The High Holydays

Every autumn the Jewish people observe what are known as the High Holydays.

This is a period of ten days beginning with Rosh Hashanah, which means New Year, and ending with Yom Kippur, the Day of Atonement.

The Jewish New Year has nothing to do with the calendar year. Jews regard January the First as the beginning of the regular year, as everyone else does.

The term, new year, is used by the Jews at this time to mean the new effort which they make to correct mistakes they may have made in the past. It is a new year of conscience, not the calendar.

Actually, the time when we get going all over again on duties and tasks temporarily suspended is the autumn. That's when school starts after the summer vacation; that's when organizations start their activities again. It's a more logical break in the year than January the First.

At that important time, when the summer is over and the brisk breezes of fall begin to arouse us, the Jewish people take time out to try to stir themselves to improve the quality of their deeds.

They do this at worship services in their synagogues. They recite prayers thanking God for giving men and women the power to tell right from wrong. They sit silently and think about the errors they may have committed. They sing hymns in which the idea of forgiving others is emphasized. They listen to the rabbi who reminds them that believing in God means trying to make use of the powers for goodness and mercy which are deposited in all of us, but which we sometimes neglect. They hearken to the Shofar, which is a ram's horn, with a rousing sound, designed to awaken the conscience that might be slumbering.

On the tenth day of this period of penitence, or repentance, there takes place the observance of the Day of Atonement.

As recommended in the Book of Leviticus of the Bible (Chap. 23), the Day of Atonement is a day of fasting. Fasting makes us uncomfortable, so it makes us think of the discomfort we may have brought to others by our thoughtlessness or negligence. As with all Jewish holydays, the observance of Yom Kippur begins in the evening. The worship service then includes the singing of the hymn, Kol Nidre, which means All Vows, a plea for forgiveness for decisions made in haste and without regard for the feelings of others.

On Atonement Day the worshipper thinks of his faults and tries to atone for them; that is, realize how wrong they were and make up his mind not to repeat them. He tries hard also to feel forgiveness for those who have wronged him. The prayerbook, the songs, the sermons, the large gathering in the temple, all these lift him up to a new level of understanding and tenderness, and give him a new sense of the sacredness of life.

These days are high. That is, they lift the worshipper up in an effort to come closer to the Source of good conduct. They are holy, because nothing is more sacred than improving the relationship between people.

When the High Holydays are over, Jews wish one another a happy new year of the spirit. They say to one another, Good Yomtov, which means Happy Holiday. Or, they say, L'shanah Tovah, which is Hebrew for Happy New Year.

Although the Jewish High Holydays are the most important religious occasion for the Jewish people, there is nothing about the holydays which does not apply to all people. That is why one rabbi once told his congregation, the way that we can really **atone** is to strive to be **at one** with everyone.

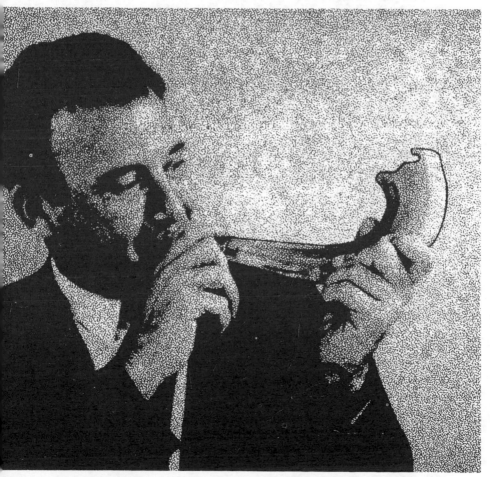

The Shofar is sounded on the High Holydays and whenever the conscience of mankind is to be aroused. The Shofar is a ram's horn.

Canned goods are often brought to the Jewish religious school on the holiday of Sukkot and then distributed to the needy on Thanksgiving.

Sukkot

The holiday of Sukkot is one of the ways that the Jewish people say thank-you to God. It is a holiday which comes in the autumn when nature is very pretty: with browns, yellows, reds, violets, and purples on the trees and in the fields. Thousands of years ago the Jewish farmers created this holdiay because they wanted to say thanks to the Lord for the beauty around them and because it was a time when they rested up a bit before they got to work on gathering in the autumn harvest.

In your Bible you can read about Sukkot in the Book of Leviticus, Chapter 23, the Book of Exodus, Chapter 23; and in the Book of Numbers, Chapter 29.

Sukkot is a Hebrew word which means tents or huts. The holiday is connected also with the time when the Jews were in the desert. For forty years they lived in tents as they traveled to the land of freedom, and during all that time the Lord protected them. So they declared a holiday, which they called Sukkot, huts, sometimes known as Tabernacles.

Sukkot stands for so many things that it is celebrated a whole week, or eight days by more traditional Jews. An extra day has been added, too. It is called Simchat Torah, the Joy of Learning, and on that day the last chapters of the Books of Moses are read in the Synagogue, and immediately, the first chapters are read, to show that one must never stop learning to do the right thing.

On Sukkot it is the custom to build a hut, outside one's home, or in or near the synagogue, to remind one that the ancient Jews actually lived in these skimpy things as they marched towards freedom. The hut, or sukkah, is open at the top, so that one can see the sky, and it is decorated with the fruits and foliage of the autumn season. The little hut also reminds us of the fact that many people do not have decent houses in which to live. Sukkot is, therefore, a time when people are urged to make gifts to the poor and help to find ways of putting an end to poverty.

Our Thanksgiving Day in the United States was modeled after Sukkot by the Pilgrims who loved the Bible. The Pilgrims felt that they were like the Jews of olden times because they, too, left a land of bondage, wandered over unknown territory towards a land of promise and freedom. So, when they got over a very hard time, they proclaimed a feast of thanks to God, like Sukkot. They were going to make Thanksgiving on Sunday, but they wanted it to be separate from their own Sabbath. They thought of making it on Saturday, but they remembered that was the Jewish Sabbath. They decided not to make it on Friday either, for that is the Mohammedan Sabbath. So they chose Thursday, a day when people of all faiths could have an extra celebration. Sukkot and Thanksgiving remind us that we prove how mature we are by the speed with which we say thanks and by the ways we show our gratitude for the many blessings we enjoy.

Chanukah

When Christmas begins to effervesce on all sides, all Americans are now aware of a Jewish winter festival which often adjoins Christmas on the calendar, and is sometimes erroneously referred to as the "Jewish Christmas." Chanukah is a holiday in its own right and has behind it an intriguing story.

Pronounced with a gargle, Chanukah is a Hebrew word meaning Dedication. The holiday, observed for eight days is so called because it commemorates the reconstruction of the ancient temple in Judea some 165 years before the Christian era.

The sanctuary had to be rededicated because it had been contaminated by the Syrian minions of a monarch named Antiochus. Heir, by several removes, of one-third of the empire of Alexander the Great, Antiochus had decreed that all of his subjects must pay him taxes and also adopt his kind of idolatry.

Everyone within his hegemony did as Antiochus commanded except for the inhabitants of tiny Judea. Taxes they would pay, but bend the knee to the molten gods the Judeans would not.

The result was one of the most lopsided conflicts in history. The small Judean forces, led by the redoubtable Judah Maccabee and his four brothers, seemed to have nary a chance to stand off the world's mightiest military force.

But stand them off they did. In three years of warfare, during which for the first time in battlefield annals, guerilla tactics were employed, the tough Judeans defeated their far more numerous foes. To do this they had to cope with the first recorded use of elephants as

Telling the Chanukah story to youngsters, as the nine-branched Chanukah candelabrum waits to be lit.

military devices. To do this they had to get rabbinical authority to violate the Sabbath, for the sly Syrians kept attacking on the Jewish rest day until the Judeans decided it was better to live on their feet than die on their knees. To do this they had to be inspired to incredible heights of intrepidity by the cause which enlisted their efforts.

Victorious, the Judeans proceeded to cleanse the temple. A legend has it that the amount of oil available to kindle the Eternal Light in the sanctuary was enough for only one day, but miraculously endured for eight days. The legend is a dramatic way of saying that a good cause, upheld at first by few, will win augmented support if zealously pursued. The holiday is observed for eight days, with an additional taper lit in the holiday candelabrum each night.

Special prayers and songs, gift-giving and contributions to charity, reminders of the debt we owe to the valor of freedom fighters of all ages, are all rehearsed in synagogue and home.

The festival hymn called "Rock of Ages," salutes God's "arm" and looks towards the total disappearance of tyranny. A Chanukah prayer calls upon the worshipper to "battle against apathy, ignorance and intolerance which still threaten to extinguish Thy lamps and to destroy Thine altars." The holiday candelabrum contains not eight lights, but nine. The ninth candle is called "The Servant Candle," symbolizing the Jew's mandate to add light and enlightenment to society.

Did the Chanukah story actually take place? Yes, it did. The saga is chronicled in the Books of the Maccabees, part of the post-Biblical series of narratives known as the Apocrypha. Coins bearing the name of Simon the Maccabee have been unearthed in the holy land. Is it possible for a few Judeans to have triumphed over so might a host? Skeptics should remember George Washington, The R.A.F. vs. the Luftwaffe, and the exploits of the fighting Jews of Israel, the latter-day Maccabeans who held off seven Arab nations determined to bash them into the sea.

During the festive and uplifting Christmas season, many Jews are swirled into the holiday's orbit. This is understandable. It would also make sense for Christians to share in the Chanukah spirit, for were it not for the bravery of those who gave the world Chanukah, monotheism as a faith might have disappeared and Judaism would have lacked the vigor to give birth to Christianity 165 years following the Maccabean events. And Christians need only turn to the Tenth Chapter of the Book of John to learn that Jesus celebrated the Feast of Dedication (or the Feast of Lights, as it sometimes is known).

The first recorded struggle for freedom of conscience in the annals of history, Chanukah merits the decent respect of all who cherish the light of liberty.

Purim

Purim, merriest of Jewish holidays, occurs either in February or March.

The word Purim means "lots" and refers to the manner in which an ancient Persian bigot, Haman by name, decided on what day to carry out his plan to get rid of the Jewish people. The story is to be found in the Book of Esther in the Bible.

Haman's wrath was kindled by the refusal of Mordecai the Jew to bow down to him or his effigy. Sensing that the Jewish faith was hostile to his dictatorship Haman planned to eliminate the Jews.

How this plot was thwarted through an act of patriotism on the part of Mordecai and by the courageous intercession of Esther, Mordecai's cousin, who becomes Queen of Persia, is the story line of the Biblical volume.

The joyousness of the holiday observance, which expresses itself through song and prayers of thanksgiving, derives from the relief felt each year over the triumph over tyranny. Gift-giving and giving to the poor also mark the day.

In temples and synagogues, the Esther story is read from a special scroll called megillah, at a special service. In religious schools, pageants and plays rehearse the story and at homes special feasts further underscore the jolly spirit of the day.

"Don't tell me you're expecting still another Jewish holiday," said Paul to his neighbor's mother, Mrs. Baker. "Seems every time you turn around another Jewish holiday is coming."

"Well, no wonder," said Jim Baker to Paul, "Look how long the Jewish people have been around."

"How long?" asked Paul.

Jim looked up to his mother, and guessed. "Oh, millions of years!"

"No, not millions," said Mrs. Baker, "but several thousand."

"And what's the name of the new holiday that's coming up?" Paul wanted to know.

"Purim," replied Jim.

"Purim! What's that mean? A holiday for the poor?" asked Paul.

Jim looked puzzled, "Tell you the truth, I don't know what the word does mean. But I know about the holiday. It's quite a story, isn't it, Mom?"

"It certainly is," agreed Mom.

"Well, how does it go?" demanded Paul.

"I'm not sure I can get it all straight," ventured Jim, "but it takes place in Persia."

"You mean Iran?" said Paul.

"You're a pretty smart child to know that Iran is what they now call Persia," said Mrs. Baker. "But this story happened some 3,500 years ago in the country that used to be known as Persia. And the king of that country needed a queen, so he ran a beauty contest."

"Yeh," Jim chimed in, "and the winner was a Jewish girl named Esther, who became the queen."

"Isn't there a movie about that?" asked Paul.

"Yes, there is. Did you see it?" Mrs. Baker wanted to know.

"No. I don't like movies. I went to one once, but I fell asleep. But my aunt was talking about it. And wasn't there a man in the story called Morton?"

"Today he would probably be called Morton, but then he was called Mordecai," said Mrs. Baker. "Yes, he's the hero of the story."

"And the villain is Haman. Haman was like the prime minister," Jim raced on, "and he said everybody had to bow down to him. And everybody did, except Mordecai."

"Why didn't he?" asked Paul.

"Because he would only bow down to God, not to any person. Like the Jewish religion teaches," explained Jim.

Mrs. Baker helped out, "And Paul's religion teaches that too, Jim."

"Uh..huh," said Jim, "but it took guts for Mordecai to refuse, because Haman had all the power."

Paul became curious. "And what did Haman do?"

"Haman went to the king..." began Jim.

"Do you remember his name?" asked his mother.

"You pronounce it like a sneeze," recalled Jim.

"Yes," his mother prompted, "Ahasuerus!"

"Ahas--what?" asked Paul.

"Well, it doesn't matter," said Mrs. Baker. "Haman went to the king and said to him that the Jewish people were not loyal to him and he asked permission to get rid of them."

"And what did the king say?" asked Paul.

"That dumb king said O.K.," Jim notified him. "He didn't know that his own queen was Jewish. Not only that. It also happened that the same Mordecai saved the king's life."

"How?" Paul inquired.

"A couple of murderers were planning to kill the king. By good luck Mordecai overheard them plotting and reported it to the people at the palace, and that's how his life was saved," related Jim.

"Then what happened?" asked Paul.

"Well, Mordecai was Esther's cousin. So he went to her and told her to go to the king and save the Jewish people." Jim told him.

"Yes," added Mrs. Baker, "but it wasn't so simple. You see, back in those days, a king had absolute power, and, according to the story, if he just didn't feel like talking to Esther, she might have her head chopped off."

"Now, that's pretty silly," said Paul.

"Sure," agreed Jim, "one-man rule is always silly. But that is how the story goes. So Esther risked her life to save the people."

"And did she save them?" asked Paul.

"Yes, and that's why we celebrate the holiday of Purim," said Jim.

"When we celebrate we think of Mordecai's heroism," Mrs. Baker told the boys, "and of Esther's courage."

"And how do you celebrate?" asked Paul.

"Purim is one of the jolliest holidays of all. We have a service, and during the service we are allowed to cheer for Mordecai and boo Haman. We have parties and we eat hamentashen," Jim declared.

"Hamentashen, what are they?" asked Paul.

"They're three-cornered pastries, full of jelly or something sweet," said Jim, "aren't they, Mom?"

Mom nodded. "Yes, hamentashen means Haman's pockets, but actually they're shaped like what we think his hat looked like, and as we eat them we tell ourselves we never want to be as mean as Haman was."

"Yeah, but you still haven't told me what the name of the holiday means," said Paul, "What did you say it's called: Poodim?"

"No, Purim," said Mrs. Baker. "Actually the word is Persian and it means lots."

"Because you have lots of fun?" asked Paul.

"No," smiled Mrs. Baker, "not that lots. Lots, meaning take a chance. It seems that Haman pulled lots to figure out when to get rid of the Jewish people. And it turned out that was the same day that they were saved."

"I think I get it," said Jim, "it's like pulling knots in a handkerchief. That's called lots, too."

"Yes, it is," said Mrs. Baker, "but the name of the holiday seems to tell us that it's a matter of chance when anyone might be threatened by something bad. Therefore, we should all stick together to put a stop to evil things."

Paul said, "Well, thanks for telling me about the holiday. I hope I can remember it to tell to my folks."

"You don't have to remember it in your head, Paul," Mrs. Baker said, "it's all written out in a book."

"Yeh," said Paul, "but I probably don't have a copy."

"Yes you do," smiled Mrs. Baker.

"I don't think so. I don't have any Jewish holiday book, Mrs. Baker," Paul said.

"Yes, you do, Paul. The whole story is from the Bible."

"It is?" Paul said in wonder.

"Yes," said Mrs. Baker, "you can look it up any time you want to. Just look for the Book of Esther."

"Thanks, and I hope you have a merry Purim," said Paul, as he and Jim ran off for a bit of baseball practice.

The lamb is a Passover symbol, because its gait reminds one of the sprightliness which one experiences with the arrival of Spring, which Passover celebrates.

Passover

Passover is history's first freedom festival.

Ordained in the Bible, it celebrates the exodus from Egyptian slavery.

It is also an opportunity to welcome the advent of Spring. As such it is one of the three agricultural festivals dating back to Biblical days. The others are Tabernacles (Sukkot) connected with the autumn harvest, and Pentecost (Shavuot) identified with the first fruits of the Spring planting.

Passover is observed with worship services, including special prayers glorifying liberty, the miracle of nature reborn and the inspiration which we receive from leaders who respond to the divine message about human equality.

A unique observance associated with Passover is the Seder (pronounced Sayder), which is a home worship service around the dinner table held on the first two nights of the holiday (by the Orthodox and Conservative) and on the first night (by some Reform).

The Seder is a family or communal gathering at which the events of the Exodus are remembered and during which each individual attempts to recapture the anguish of servitude and the joy of deliverance.

From a special Passover book called the Haggadah ("The Narrative") the breakaway from Pharaoh is retold. Blessings are recited. Songs are sung. Even table games are played and an atmosphere of jubilation and reverence is created. Ceremonial foods are held up and their symbolism explained: the matzah, or dried cracker, is eaten to get an idea of the meager food which the disadvantaged eat; a sprig of parsley betokens the Springtime; wine is an emblem of human sweetness; a bitter herb stands for the bitterness of slavery.

The New Testament Last Supper was a Seder (a Hebrew word meaning Order or Procedure). At that time a new significance was given to the matzah and the wine; thus originated communion or the Eucharist.

Some of the Biblical references to Passover are Exodus 12.3; Leviticus 23.4; Number 9, and Deuteronomy 16. Among the New Testament references are Matthew 26.19; Mark 14.12; Luke 22.7, and John 13.

For more information, see your nearest rabbi or Christian minister.

Passover—for Young People

You don't have to be Jewish to be glad about the Jewish holiday of Passover.

You just have to be fond of freedom.

You know what freedom is, don't you?

Freedom means the right to live where you want to, to worship as you want to, to have the respect of other people, to stay clear of being annoyed by other people, as long as you obey the laws which are passed by those elected to office.

Well, it wasn't like that for the ancient Hebrews when they lived in Egypt, as you can tell from the Bible.

The Egyptians made slaves out of them, even though one of the wisest of Egyptian Jews, Joseph, had saved the country from famine.

And the man who put a stop to this slavery was Moses, who grew up in the palace of the Pharaoh, as Egyptians called their king.

Moses was actually Jewish, but he didn't know it, for he had been brought to the palace when he was just a baby.

He lived like a prince, but when he saw slavery on all sides of him, he couldn't stand it.

And he voluntarily left his comfortable life, joined the Jews and led the revolt against Pharaoh.

It is this freeing of the Jews, or deliverance, to use a harder word, which the Jewish people celebrate with the joyous holiday of Passover.

The Jewish people, thousands of years ago, "passed over" from slavery to liberty. It was the first time in history that a fight for freedom was waged, and that is why the Jewish people are happy all over again every Spring when the festival of Passover rolls around.

The celebration lasts a week, with the first two nights and the last two, the most important.

On Passover there is a religious service, in which thanks are said to God for inspiring all those who labor to bring benefit to other people.

On the first night of Passover, and the second one too, among many Jews, there takes place in Jewish homes a festive supper in honor of Passover.

The supper is called the Seder (pronounced say-der), which means Schedule, and the schedule is very interesting.

From a book called "The Story" (in Hebrew, that's Haggadah) the things that happened in ancient Egypt are read. Then different foods are held up to make the story more dramatic.

The matzah, or unleavened bread, is held up. That's a kind of a dry cracker, eaten to give the people a taste of the unappetizing food which poor people and slaves eat. That is supposed to make the eater sympathetic with the poor and induce him to try to help them. A bitter herb is also eaten as a symbol of the bitterness of slavery.

Everyone in the family and guests at the Seder table also eat a sprig of greens to recall that Moses freed his people when the Spring of the year was coming around.

The Seder is of interest to Christians too, for that's what "The Last Supper" was.

One point in the seder calls for the youngest person there (that is, the youngest person who can talk) to ask "Four Questions" about the holiday.

There is singing at the meal, and prayers are said, and at the end there is even a game, as children look for the Afikomen (a piece of matzah which is hidden) for which the parents give prizes. The idea is to give the children a feeling of fun at the celebration.

The next morning in the synagogue, prayers, sermon and music remind one again of the importance of freedom. One prayer, for example, goes like this: "May the hunger after freedom and justice be satisfied and may all mankind be blessed with the joys of brotherhood and peace."

The last words spoken at the Seder are: "Next year at this time may all the people on earth be free."

See what we meant when we said you don't have to be Jewish to be glad about the Jewish holiday of Passover?

The agricultural background of Judaism is recalled when the holiday of Shavuot, or First Fruits, recurs. It originally commemorated the gratitude which the farmer feels when he sees the results of his spring planting.

Shavuot

The Jewish holiday called Shavuot (pronounced Sha-voo-ote) is one of three Pilgrim Festivals mentioned in the Bible.

The other two are Passover (Hebrew: Pay-sach) and Tabernacles, or Booths (Su-kot).

Originally nature festivals, these three holidays marked important milestones in the agricultural year. Passover was at first the plea to God to make the Spring harvest a good one; later it became the time to observe the deliverance from Egyptian slavery. Sukkot started as a time to mark the beginning of the autumn harvest and was later identified with the protection God granted the Israelites as, for forty years in the desert, they lived in Sukkot (tents or booths).

Shavuot means, in Hebrew, Weeks, and is the festival which takes place seven weeks after Passover, the time of the Spring planting. Those 49 days are the length of time needed for the appearance of the first results of the planting. For this reason Weeks is also called the Festival of the First Fruits. In ancient times, stalks of grain were brought to the temple in Jerusalem and there thanks were offered up to God for His part in producing the food we eat. That is the origin of the idea of pilgrimages, of trips to a holy place. As indicated, these visits to the shrine also took place on Passover and Sukkot.

Because of the fifty-day period between the holidays, the climax of this span is called not only Shavuot (Weeks) but Pentecost (related to fifty).

That fifty-day stretch later took on new significance with respect to the happenings to the Israelites after the Exodus from Egypt. According to tradition, those seven weeks in the desert were used by Moses to provide moral training to the former slaves, and this course in ethics reached a "high point" fifty days after the Exodus on Mt. Sinai where the Ten Commandments were given. Shavuot, therefore, has come to be known as the Birthday of the Ten Commandments, and one of its Hebrew names, in fact, is the Time of Giving of the Moral Law.

The holiday was celebrated for one day in Biblical times. Traditionalist Jews added another day to its observance for complex calendar reasons. Reform Jews have reverted to the original one-day pattern. In Israel, too, it is a one-day event.

But Reform Judaism utilized Shavuot for another purpose. Desirous of an occasion for a ceremony marking the completion of the elementary period of religious education, Reform Judaism combined their celebration of Shavuot with an opportunity for teenagers to assert their willingness to adhere to Jewish precepts. At the first Shavuot, near Mt. Sinai, the people affirmed their willingness to live by divine principles. On each subsequent Shavuot, young people ratify that decision; hence the ceremony is called Confirmation.

There are many practices associated with the fifty-day period between Passover and Pentecost. For one thing it is a period of extra devotion and abstention from undue revelry (like Lent, which is patterned after it). The seven-week span is called in Hebrew, Sefirah (s'feer-ah), which means Counting (count up, not count down) or Omer, which is Hebrew for the stalk of barley which is gestating during that time. The somberness of the period was broken on the thirty-third day because, according to legend, the disciples of the great Talmudist, Akiba, ceased to suffer from an epidemic on that day; so it became a half-festival, Lag B'Omer (the 33rd day during the Omer).

In Hebrew, first fruits is Bikkurim, as the holiday is sometimes called. Some refer to it as Chag (Festival of) Bikkurim. Confirmation is now prevalent not only among Reform Jews, but also among Conservative and Orthodox Jews as well.

Confirmation is to be distinguished from Bar Mitzvah (for boys), or Bas Mitzvah (for girls). Bar Mitzvah means Son of the Commandment, or Master of the Commandment, and refers to the ability of a thirteen-year old to "master" sufficient Hebrew to take part in a worship service, or perhaps to "master" some religious duties. The Bar Mitzvah or Bas Mitzvah ceremony is a "solo" achievement. Confirmation is a group exercise, for both girls and boys who have completed their elementary religious education.

References to Shavuot can be found in the Bible in Exodus 34.22, 23.16; Leviticus 23.15; and Deuteronomy 16.9. In the New Testament it is mentioned in Acts 2.1.

Tisha b'Ab

Tisha is nine, and Ab (or Av) is a Hebrew month.

This date is a memorial and fast day, commemorating not one but several calamities which are said to have occurred at this juncture in the calendar.

The misfortunes probably did not happen all on the same day, but the fashioners of Judaism sought to compress the mourning of the people into one period, instead of spreading lugubriousness through the calendar.

Tradition has it that the Ninth Day of Ab is when the Ten Tribes were taken captive in 586 B.C.E. by the Babylonians, and when a great post-milennium Jewish military hero, Bar Kochba, lost a decisive battle against the Romans.

Probably the most authentic dire happening ascribed to this date is the fall of the Jerusalem Temple in the year 70 of this era, after a long siege by the Roman general, Titus.

In observance of this day, the worship service is a sad one. Dirges (called in Hebrew kinot) are read. A Scriptural reading is Lamentations, attributed to Jeremiah, who was supposed to have witnessed the sacking of Jerusalem by the Babylonians.

In some Orthodox synagogues the ark of the Torah is draped in black, and people sit on boxes, indicative of the lowliness experienced by mourners. In Israel the Western Wall (sometimes called the Wailing Wall), all that is left of the great Jerusalem sanctuary, is the scene of special gatherings on Tisha b'Ab.

Tisha b'Ab is a day of sadness for non-Orthodox Jews as well as more traditionalist ones, but many a Reform temple omits any special liturgy on that day. The reason is theological: the Orthodox look forward to the restoration of the ancient sanctuary and its sacrificial system. Reform holds that the catastrophe was indeed horrid, but it had the result of sending the Jewish people out into the world, there to minister to the rest of society in accordance with the "mission idea" fostered by the Hebrew prophets. That idea does not call for prosyletization of others, just their spiritualization.

The famed Arch of Titus, announcing to the residents of Rome that "Judea Capta," that Judea was captured. Jews wouldn't go under it until 1948, when Judea was resurrected.

Chamisha Asar Bishvat

Chamisha Asar Bishvat means "Fifteen in Shvat."

Shvat is a Hebrew month, and on the fifteenth of that month a minor Jewish festival occurs. It Is the equivalent of our Arbor Day and is known in the Talmud as "The New Year of the Trees."

The holiday is the occasion in Israel of tree plantings; the reforestation program there has been phenomenal.

It is also a time when picnics and outings occur. The mini-holiday underlines the need to admire nature and to appreciate the glory of the physical world, which we realize now is being tarnished.

In the United States and elsewhere it has become a practice to mark this holiday by the purchase of trees in Israel to aid the cause of the National Jewish Fund in making the Holy Land blossom again.

A food associated with Chamisha Asar Bishvat is St. John's Bread, known in Yiddish as bokser.

The Jewish Calendar

In order to understand the Jewish religious calendar, we have to refresh our memory with regard to the definitions of a day, a month and a year.

A day is the time that it takes the earth to revolve on its axis, 24 hours.

A month, as the name implies, is the time it takes the moon to circle the earth, which is 29 days, 12 hours, 44 minutes and three seconds.

A year is the time it takes the earth to go about the sun, which is 365 days, 5 hours, 48 minutes and 46 seconds.

It is obvious that the days do not divide equally into the months or the years. Hence, if we have a solar calendar, we must make some adjustments. These adjustments are effectuated through additions of days to the years at various intervals. Our adjustments are leap days every fourth year, except for some of the even years marking the beginning of centuries.

The computation of the annual cycles of the moon and the sun goes back to the days of the Egyptians. Our solar calendar came to us from them through the Romans, who made two refinements in it in the reign of Julius Caesar and Augustus. Finally Pope Gregory introduced other improvements. Hence our calendar is called the Gregorian Calendar. It modified the Julian calendar which, in turn, had introduced changes in the so-called Ptolemian Calendar.

The purpose of a calendar is to mark off certain intervals and to keep a systemic record of recurrent events, enabling us to have a trustworthy means of reckoning dates in advance, as well as fixing certain civil or religious occasions.

For the ancient Hebrews, the later Israelites and the modern Jews, a fixed calendar was essential.

Therefore, from the earliest times, computation of the time of important observances was a necessity for the Jewish people.

For one thing it was vital to celebrate the Sabbath on time. The Sabbath represented a halt in the mad rush of economic materialism; hence it must be correctly celebrated. It was not enough just to count the days and rest at the end of the week. It was important to know exactly when the Sabbath began. So, early in Jewish history, the calculations were made as precise as possible.

To the Jew the day begins at sunset. This notion has a historic and a theological basis. In the opening words of the Bible, the Creation story includes the litany, at the end of the work done by the Creator on each day: "It was evening, and it was morning." Evening is mentioned first. Hence the day was regarded as beginning at sunset. Philosophically this was interpreted as meaning that when things look black or bleak we must not think the end has come. No, the darkness is the prelude to the dawn. If man is creative, as the Lord was, the darkness will precede the morning.

But the Sabbath began with the appearance of the moon. It was therefore important to know when the moon was first visible. This led to the study and scrutiny of the heavens.

This examination of the moon was even more important in ancient days because amongst Jews there grew up the practice of making the arrival of the New

Moon into a holiday. So appreciative were the Israelites of the recurrent miracle of the advent of the moon, so awesome did this gift of God seem to them that they celebrated the arrival of the new moon whenever it occurred. The arrival was accompanied by the recitation of a prayer of thanksgiving. The rhythm of nature, as exemplified in the predictable return of the moon, gave rise to added faith in the reliability of God.

Supremely significant to the Jew was the appearance of the new moon on the seventh month of the year. Perhaps seven has always been associated with good luck. The seventh month in the Jewish calendar coincided with the conclusion of summer, and also with the autumnal equinox. The year was commencing all over again, after its summer splurge. The seasons were beginning their annual pirouette. It was a good time to marvel afresh at the constancy of God's management of the universe. Gradually that new moon of the seventh month, the month which brought autumn to the world, became a day of solemnity par excellence to the Jew. He fashioned a legend to the effect that the world had been created at that time. He told his children that the recurrence of that day was a sign that man, made in the image of God, could also find new sources of creativity each year.

That special new moon of the seventh month (called Tishri) came to be known as the Head of the Year. The Hebrew Rosh Hashanah, is often called the New Year. It became a day of reflection, of review, of repentance, and gradually in Jewish history it became the first day of a skein of 10 days given over to self-examination and penance. The climax of the period of penitence was designated as Yom Kippur, the tenth day of the Month of Tishri, the Day of Atonement, a twenty-four hour span given over to prayer, forgiveness, and fasting.

It became extremely vital to pin-point the arrival of the New Year, for the calendation of the rest of the year rested upon the exactitude of determining the beginning. In ancient Palestine individuals who spotted the moon would report their findings to the priestly authorities. The latter would send up flares or beacons, and a series of relayed flares on high places and mountain-tops would convey the data to the rest of the country.

Later, when the Jews wandered beyond Palestine, messengers would carry the tidings. Gradually, in lands outside of Palestine, it became customary to celebrate the holydays on two days instead of one just in case there was a mistake.

To this day, traditionalist Jews celebrate Rosh Hashanah for two days as a record of the difficulties of being sure, in those early times, that the moon had really been spotted. Reform Jews have reverted to the one-day observance.

But, of course, the fast day of Yom Kippur is observed but one day by all, for it was contrary to the humanitarianism of Judaism to countenance the prolongation of a foodless period.

Indeed, this humanitarianism prompted further astronomical research on the part of the Israelites. Because the Sabbath was a day of rest when one was supposed to abstain from all labor, including cooking, it was decided that Yom Kippur must never occur on a

Friday or a Sunday, for if you fasted on Friday, you'd be unable to cook a meal on Saturday, and if you observed the Sabbath by refraining from cooking and then had to approach a fast day on Sunday, you'd be famished two days running. It was also decreed that Rosh Hashanah must also never fall on Friday or Sunday, for if either occurred it would have caused difficulties on other holidays in the course of the year.

Additional motivation for Jewish interest in astronomy and in the precise computation of the days of the calendar is to be found in the nature of other Jewish holidays.

Aside from Rosh Hashanah and Yom Kippur, known now as the High Holydays, the major Jewish observances are three in number. These holidays originated in the agricultural activities of the ancient Jewish farmers. One of these days is Passover, which roughly coincides with the advent of Spring and which was associated with the Spring harvest. Another is Tabernacles, known in Hebrew as Su-kose, (Sukkot) which is the time for thanksgiving for the autumn harvest and which is, incidentally, the actual model after which the Pilgrims patterned our American Thanksgiving Day. The third festival is known as Pentecost, or Sha-voo-ote (Shavuot) in Hebrew, and it celebrates the appearance of the first fruits after the spring planting. It is called Pentecost because it occurs fifty days after Passover. Shavuot is Hebrew for "weeks."

Obviously, these holidays had to be celebrated at the same time each year. They were identified with specific intervals in the life of the farmer and they couldn't slide through the year.

The holidays would have done a lot of sliding if the Israelites had clung to the lunar calendar. Often the Hebrew calendar is described as lunar. It was based on the moon, true, but early in Jewish history it was adjusted to the cycle of the sun.

To see what happens if an unadjusted lunar rhythm is permitted to hold sway we merely have to gaze at the Mohammedan calendar. It is purely lunar and, from the point of view of periodicity, almost looney. For various holidays occur during different seasons as the years go by. If we were on a lunar calendar, Christmas would gradually veer towards the summer and Easter would gradually find its way towards the wintry months.

The reason for this has already been stated. The solar year is 365 days plus; the lunar cycle is approximately 15 days shorter. The Hebrew calendar is not lunar; a long time ago it became what is known as luni-solar, or a bound, lunar calendar. Adjustments were made to correlate the two divergent cycles.

The process of reconciliation is quite complicated. A 19-year cycle was the basis of the operation. During that 19-year period, days were added to months and, at certain intervals, an entire month was added.

In our solar calendar when we say we have a leap year, we know that one day, February 29, has been tacked on to the year.

But in the Jewish calendar a leap year is one in which an entire month was added. This month is interpolated seven times during the 19-year spread. It happens in these years: the 3rd, the 6th, the 8th, the 11th, the 14th, the 17th and the 19th.

The inserted month is of 30 days. It has the same name as the month it follows, except that it is called the Second. The intercalation, as it is called, is of the month which comes just before the month which contains the festival of Passover. This was done, of course, to make sure that the spring holiday came out in the Spring. The added month is known as Adar Two (or the Second).

Because of certain requirements in the calendar we can see that the length of the Jewish religious year can vary.

The New Year must not begin on a Friday or a Sunday, as has been indicated. It may not begin on a Wednesday, because there is also a prohibition against permitting the 7th day of the Festival of Tabernacles, the autumn holiday which occurs shortly after the High Holydays, to fall on a Saturday.

So we can see the complications. If the new moon of the seventh month is scheduled to take place on Monday, Tuesday, Thursday, or Saturday, then Rosh Hashanah is permitted to occur at that time. Such a year, if it is not a leap year, will contain 353 days, and will be a lunar year.

If the new moon of the seventh month is slated to take place on a Wednesday, Friday, or a Sunday, the celebration of the New Year is postponed by one day, and that year, if not a leap year, will last a day longer, that is 354 days.

There is one other provision which can lengthen the Jewish year. If the lunar conjunction which marks the beginning of the new year is scheduled to occur after the noon hour, the beginning of the year is put ahead one day. Now, if that move should cause the year to begin on one of the forbidden days, the year is actually moved **two** days. Some years are, therefore 355 days in length.

These differences are accommodated by varying the length of some of the months of the year. There are twelve months in the non-leap year. In years with 354 days some of these months are given 29 days; if the year must be a bit longer, they are given 30 days. The months which thus fluctuate are always the same ones: they are the 8th and 9th months.

Now, we can readily see that when the leap month is added to balance the lunar and solar cycles, the year can either be 383 days long, or 384 or 385.

The basis for the 19-year lunar cycle is the research done by an Athenian scholar named Meton in 432 B.C.E. It was Meton who modified the Athenian calendar, and the Jewish authorities adopted his method of calculations. For this reason the cycle is often called the Metonic cycle. The longer years are called Embolismic, or swollen.

In the earliest days the Israelite authorities would annually announce the advent of the new year. Later the calculations were fixed, but they were kept secret, and the officials would make the announcements in advance. When the Jewish people were dispersed in 70 C.E., the leadership was transferred to certain scholarly individuals who flourished in Babylonia, which is now Iraq. These patriarchs, or sages, were granted the power by virtue of their learning to regulate the religious lives of their people. In 359 C. E.

one of these leaders, whose name was Hillel II, published the complex and intricate system whereby the calender was computed, so that Jewish communities everywhere could do their own reckoning. This procedure announced by Hillel still prevails to day.

Actually, however, the Hillel calendar is a bit askew. The year really endures a few minutes longer than was believed in those times. For this reason, the lunar segment of the Jewish calendar is gradually moving ahead within the solar segment. The pace of this advance is about 4 days in a thousand years. This means that Jews now celebrate Passover, the spring holiday, 4 days later than was the case 1000 years ago. The march of Passover into the month of May will eventually cause an unbalance, if it is not checked. Now that the State of Israel has come into being there is a considerable agitation among some rabbis for the convocation of a rabbinical council, or a Jewish ecumenical body like the one which met in Rome, to authorize the necessary changes which will check the inaccuracies in the Jewish calendar.

As is known, the number of the Jewish year harks back to the theoretical time of Creation as it has been figured out from the Biblical accounts. That is not to say that Jews really think the world began in 3760 B.C.E., but it became a ready way of numbering the years and has been adopted. The Jewish New Year which began September, 1971 is thus numbered 5732. In the Bible, years were hitched to various events like the Exodus and the Babylonian Exile, but later on the practice of reckoning the year from the hypothetical date of 3760 B.C.E. came into vogue.

According to this hypothetical scheme, Creation took place in the year 1, Noah flourished in the year 1057,

Abraham was born in 1949, the Exodus took place in the year 2449, and Christianity was born around the year 3758. Of course, we know that because of the shifts in the calendar from the Julian to the Gregorian set-up, our historians have been compelled to record the paradoxical circumstance that Jesus was born in the year 4 **B.C.E.**

A Christian involvement in the luni-solar annual cycle takes place every year in the matter of the holiday of Easter. No one has to ask, "When does Christmas occur this year?" but everyone has to ask, "When is Easter?" The reason for the question is that Easter continues to be a date hitched to the lunar calendar. Traditionally, Easter was linked to Passover, for shortly after the Last Supper, which was the celebration of the Passover, Jesus is said to have died, and, according to the New Testament, the rise of Jesus took place three days later.

The Christian Council of Nicea, in the Fourth century, one of the early ecumenical convocations, made some changes in the dating of Easter. The burden of their efforts was to separate Easter from Passover, even as church councils decreed that the Christian Sabbath should be Sunday instead of Saturday. The two holidays still come close to one another, but they do not now coincide with regard to the first day of Passover. Let us make that clear: Passover is a holiday which lasts seven days; it is now observed eight days in accordance with the practice of adding a day to the festivals outside of Palestine. The Nicean ukase forbids the first day of Passover and Easter from occurring on the same date, although very often Easter Sunday does fall within the week of Passover. The church council ruled that Easter must take place on a

Sunday after the spring equinox. Actually, we see here a recognition of the fact that Easter, like Passover, is related to the spring holiday. Similarly, Christmas and the Jewish winter holiday of Chanukah, although their purposes differ, also seem to stem back to a common source, a prehistoric mid-winter festival. As the days grew shorter and shorter, primitive man feared that perhaps there would be no more light. Hence, he sent up beacons signalling to the gods that he would like to avoid being blacked out. This practice, associated with the winter equinox, gave rise in all early cultures, to a festival of lights. It is that aspect of light that both Christmas and Chanukah have in common, although, as we have pointed out, the associations which were added to both holidays differed sharply from both their early sources and from one another.

An interesting question remains. In fact, many interesting questions remain and this superficial treatment has not at all delved deeply into the astronomical particulars surrounding the process of computation and harmonization of the lunar and solar cycles. The interesting question that we can deal with is this one. We have explained that the Jewish new year begins with the month of Tishri, but that month, it has been said, is the seventh one. Why should the year begin with the seventh month?

The answer is that there are indications that originally the year began with the fifteenth day of the month of Nisan (pronounced Nis-san), the month which contains Passover. It is logical to regard the year as beginning in the spring. It is, in fact, much more logical than beginning the year on January 1, which, although it is close to the winter equinox, has no other stigmata which imply the natural commencement of the year.

So the historians are quite certain that the Jewish year once began in the spring. Indeed, we are sure that this was the case, for Nisan is numbered Month No. 1.

The reason for the shift, however, from Nisan to Tishri, Month No. 7, is the gradual development of Judaism from a faith which dwelt exclusively upon physical nature to an outlook on life which pondered the miracle of human nature.

This evolution is visible in the manner in which the Jewish holidays were slowly elevated in their significance. Whereas their agricultural associations remained, gradually the Jewish religious leaders attached new reasons for each of the festivals.

Beginning with Passover, the weeklong feast which was originally associated with the arrival of spring, the rabbis invested its observance with a new meaning. It became the commemoration of the insurrection against slavery led by Moses. So Passover acquired a new aim; it was the birthday of freedom, for the revolt by Moses marked the first time in history that human bondage was condemned as a contravention of God's gift of liberty for all.

Similarly, the nature festival which took place fifty days after Passover underwent significant alteration or enrichment. At first it was just the celebration of the emergence of the first blossoms of the spring planting. Later the holiday was attached to the Exodus, too. Fifty days after leaving Egypt, the ex-slaves reached Mount Sinai, and there they received the Commandments, the moral law. So Pentecost became the birthday of the Ten Commandments, not merely the birthday of the first fruits of the fields and farms. In Israel it is celebrated for one day and outside of Israel, for two days.

The same process took place with respect to the autumn holiday which, you recall, is called Tabernacles, or Sukkot. It came to be regarded not only as the celebration of the harvest, but also the time to remember that those same liberated slaves lived for forty years in tabernacles, or tents, as they wandered through the desert from serfdom to freedom. So a highly spiritual note was added to the original bucolic one. In the Bible the holiday is ordained to last seven days; an additional day was tacked on outside the Holy Land.

Thus it was with the New Year. It was deliberately shifted from springtime to another period, to dramatize the fact that the new year ought to be an occasion not only for rejoicing over what happens in the soil but also for what can happen in the soul. This shiftover pointed up the religious lesson that what really matters in life is not so much the material as the moral.

It should be pointed out that Jews do not live by their religious calendar except in the matter of observing the holidays. For all other purposes, Jews live their lives by the civil calendar. This is also true in the State of Israel, where the months of January to December are utilized by the government and the people for all their regular transactions. But the religious calendar, that blend of the moon's circuit and the earth's movements, is utilized for those occasions when the people feel prompted to bless and thank Almighty God.

Bar Mitzvah

Considering how old Judaism is (it began with Abraham some 4,000 years ago), Bar Mitzvah is virtually an innovation, a "reform" in the Jewish liturgy, having been introduced in about the 13th century of this era.

At that time, or perhaps earlier, young men near their 13th birthday, were "called up" to participate in the worship service.

The boy thus marks the completion of one stage of his religious education. Part of every Sabbath service is a reading from the first five books of the Bible, which are contained in a parchment Scroll. Both the Scroll and its contents are called Torah, a Hebrew word which means instruction.

In the Torah Scroll the Hebrew words are written without vowels. By reading them from the Scroll and reciting the blessings before and after the Torah reading, the youngster demonstrates the results of his studies. The event is therefore a reason for celebration.

The 13-year-old boy is termed a Bar Mitzvah. Bar means "son of", or "expert in" in a language called Aramaic, which is related to Hebrew. Aramaic was the spoken tongue of the Judeans around the turn of the Millennium; it was the language which Jesus spoke.

Mitzvah means "commandment" or "good deed."

Bar Mitzvah then means a young man who is beginning to reach the point when he can gain satisfaction from the performance of worthy deeds. In an Orthodox setting the Bar Mitzvah is counted as one of the ten men needed to start a prayer service.

The ceremony at which the Bar Mitzvah appears is also referred to as Bar Mitzvah.

In addition to reading from one of the first five books of the Bible, the Bar Mitzvah reads an assigned part of another Biblical book. The second Scriptural reading is called Haftarah ("additional passage") and it too is preceded and followed by special blessings.

In traditional synagogues (Conservative and Orthodox) every youth is expected to become a Bar Mitzvah. In Reform synagogues it is optional, representing the willingness of the young man to undertake an assignment over and beyond the regular curriculum of the religious school.

In Reform synagogues the young man is expected to continue his studies and, some years later, he and his classmates are "inducted" into Judaism in a ceremony called Confirmation.

A ceremony introduced in modern times is the Bas Mitzvah ("daughter of the Commandment"), a Bar Mitzvah ceremony for girls.

The Torah (i. e., the first five books of the Bible) is divided into weekly sections to comprise a year's reading. The Bar Mitzvah's Torah reading is a segment of the reading-of-the-week (known in Hebrew as sedra, section, or parasha, portion).

The Torah and the Haftarah are usually linked together by an idea or contents common to each.

Interfaith Marriages

Of course interfaith marriages can work, but it's a hard row to hoe.

In this age of ecumenism, which is another word for free and easy commingling, one expects love to cross religious lines.

But because people of varying backgrounds can fall in love doesn't mean that they can stay in love.

What I have just written about the relationship between falling in love and remaining in love is true about any couple.

But if you choose a partner from another faith you are doubling the risks of marital failure. The marriage fatality rate is said to be one out of four. The rate for intermarriages has been cited as one out of two.

So one should ponder deeply the hazards and obstacles involved in crossing religious or racial matrimonial lines.

Of course, many who read this have already committed themselves to a future mate. And you who have made this decision are absolutely certain that you will make a "go" of your marriage.

How do I know this? I know it because I meet dozens of young men and women who have fallen in love and are sure that nothing in the world will make them "fall out" again.

Fine. But as you anticipate so many other eventualities in your future life it would be well for you to plan your religious future also.

This warning should be added to others you have received. Young people who are susceptible to a trans-

religious marriage are often those to whom religion means little.

"Neither of us is religious, so why should religion become a factor in our lives?" is the way the question is often put.

Well, if religion doesn't mean much to you, and you would like to keep it that way, the best thing you can do is to marry someone of your own faith. Two Christians often have little occasion to think about religion, except for the big holidays. Two Jews can virtually rule religion out of their lives, if that's the way they want it (except for the big holydays).

But when you are intermarried, religion, which you would like to keep in the background, intrudes itself into the foreground. When you are going steady, your friends comment about it. When you are engaged, your parents may get into hassles about it. When you plan your ceremony, you will become all exercised about its religious (or non-religious) nature. After you are married, the subject of religion looms up in many ways. Each holiday, large or small, can be another pinprick. When the children come, then you are really in a dither.

So I repeat: people to whom religion means little would do well to marry someone of their own creed. Then they can prevent it from becoming Topic A.

Often those who contemplate intermarriage base their sectarian decisions on the wellbeing of future children.

But the problem should be ironed out not in terms of putative offspring but in terms of the welfare of the couple itself.

There are no hard and fast rules in this situation. Each case is separate and distinct, and you would do well, if you are in this category, to have a chat with a religious leader as soon as possible. Indeed, it would be advisable to see more than one minister or priest or rabbi. Remember, the clergy is not unanimous on this matter either. You will get all kinds of counsel. Listen to everyone, and then reason out your own conclusions.

In the event that one of the partners in an interfaith romance has a stronger attachment to religion than the other, it might be well for the one with weaker loyalties to transfer to the faith of the other.

I say that because it is easier to resolve the dilemmas of mixed background if the couple opts for one faith. Many couples, ostensibly broadminded, have a different outlook. They put it this way very often: "We respect each other's faith. My fiance will remain a member of his group and I will continue to be what I am. And when we have children we will let them choose the religion they prefer."

Sounds plausible and reasonable. And in some instances the arrangement proves successful.

But in many cases it just doesn't work out. Husband and wife ought to be more united; to have each linked to a different set of sanctities pulls them apart. As for the children, they are in no position to vote for a faith. They should grow up naturally in a religious milieu provided for them by their parents. But if their parents are divided religiously, the children often face schizophrenia.

Daddy has one faith, and Mommy another. In one institution the children may be told that those who do not subscribe to its precepts are "not saved," or even "doomed." So the children are led to believe that one of their own parents is somehow "different" from them. This may estrange them from one to whom they should be ineradicably bound.

So a good rule of thumb is that one family is big enough for one religion. Hence, it may be advisable, as I have said, for the couple to choose one form of religion, preferably the one which has the stronger claim on at least one of the partners. Then the children will grow up in an environment which will be normal and not abnormal.

Of course, the children will soon sense the fact that their parents have diverse precedents. For, after all, they will have two sets of grandparents. As one youngster, product of an intermarriage said in December when we have Christmas and Chanukah. "I have some grandparents who are trees and I have some who are candles."

For those couples who have no strong link with their ancestral faith but who derive from different backgrounds, an interesting adventure would be, during the engagement period, to go "church shopping." On Friday nights, Saturday mornings and Sunday mornings, let them go to various worship services to investigate them and to see if any of them has a special appeal. Then the couple may opt for the religion of its choice. That kind of looksee is certainly more practical for mature people than for children.

Someone, of course, has to officiate at your marriage. If you have reached a religious impasse you can always have a civil ceremony, a reception, and defer the religious decision. The policies of Christian and

Jewish clergymen with respect to officiating at interreligious ceremonies vary from person to person (from "parson to parson"?). As we know, the position of the Roman Catholic church has undergone alterations in recent years. But the procedure in any diocese depends on the views of the bishop in charge. And all bishops do not agree on procedures. Protestant spiritual leaders are also far from unanimous vis-a-vis interfaith ceremonies. The policies of rabbis also reflect a wide range.

If you are in this situation and have no minister of your own, you may get in touch with me and I will be happy to chat with you about it.

Highlights of the Jewish Wedding Ceremony

1. Sipping of wine signifying the sweetness of affection.

2. A series of blessings (brochot) invoking divine blessing on the couple.

3. The placing of the ring on the finger of the spouse with the statement: "Be thou consecrated unto me...in accordance with the teachings of the faith of Israel."

4. The groom's breaking of a glass, commemorating the destruction of the Temple in Jerusalem and the need for the couple to make their home a sanctuary reflecting the ideals of that shrine. The glass is also a symbol of the fragility of human relationships and the need for tenderness in preserving them.

5. The use of a canopy (chuppah), which is like a miniature home.

Some of these practices are omitted in some Conservative and Reform weddings.

When you're talking English, you're talking Hebrew

There's that play by Moliere in which a tutor explains to the nouveau riche that there are two styles of locution: prose and poetry. After a while, the man says: "Here I've been speaking prose all my life, and I didn't know it."

People who speak English are talking a lot of Hebrew, even though many do not know it.

True, the English language, which contains many words from Latin and German, has not borrowed very extensively from Hebrew. Still there are many Hebrew terms in English.

Hebrew is especially evident in American names of people and places. As a consequence, if this country of ours were dug up thousands of years from now by archeologists it would be immediately evident that this nation enjoyed a strong Hebraic stamp.

For example, as the names of some of our presidents would be excavated, it would be seen that some first and last names derive from Hebrew. Benjamin Harrison's first name is pure Hebrew; James Abram Garfield's middle name is also Hebrew, as is Dwight David Eisenhower's. Adams is also Hebrew. The surest tell-tale name would be John, the first name of many of our presidents; and the patronymic, Johnson, in the case of two others.

It is interesting indeed that the two most common first names in our society, John and Mary, are both from the language which gave us the Torah.

The reason the h is found in John (even though it is not pronounced) is that it represents the Hebrew guttural sound, ch. The first two letters of John are one of the many abbreviations for the name of God. So John stands for Yo-chan, or the Lord is gracious. People who know Yiddish know the word, chan, meaning grace or beauty. It is the base of the name Hannah or its shortened version, Anna, with all its variations.

So if you're a Johnson or a John and someone addresses you, he is talking Hebrew.

If you're a Jon without the h, you too have a Hebrew name, for then your name is a shortened form of Yo-nathan, (Jonathan), which means the Lord gave. Nathan, he gave, is pure Hebrew. The noun form is familiar to those who speak Yiddish: mattanah, a gift.

And if your last name is Jones you too have a name taken from the Hebrew, for Jones originally meant belonging to John.

As for Mary, that's virtually Hebrew too. The lengthened form is Miriam, and the word comes from the Hebrew for bitter. In modern Hebrew a mriri is a person who is embittered.

In their general conversation, Americans mouth a lot of Hebrew when they pronounce the names of places or people or even certain English words. A good way to start the study of Hebrew would be to discover the meaning of those words which are part of our general speech.

For example, if you could ascertain the meaning of a host of extremely familiar sounds you constantly voice you would have a working vocabulary of some 200 Hebrew words.

Almost every day you say words derived from the Hebrew words for princess, escort, high, house, thanks, ram, beloved, ox, twin, heal, stalk, judge, and life.

Let's examine these terms, which are merely illustrative of the wealth of Americanisms which contain Hebraisms.

Princess.   That's what Sarah means. The masculine is sar, a Hebrew term which means chief of. The related verb means to rule or rule over, and is to be found in Israel.

Escort   in Hebrew is the verb lavah. From that verb we get the name of the assistant priest, the Levite, who escorted the cohen, the principal officiant at the Temple. From lavah we get Levi, Levine, Levinson, etc. The Hebrew word for funeral, Ivayah, and the Hebrew word for loan, Halvaah, are related. So are those jeans called Levis.

High   in Hebrew is Rahm, which you say whenever you say Abram. The word, ab, as most people know, is the Hebrew word for father. So ahvrahm (Abram) means "exalted father".   Abraham means father of a multitude.

House   in Hebrew is buy-it. If you want to say the house of, you say beth. So Beth El is the house of God, and Bethlehem is the house of bread.

Thanks   in Hebrew has a verbal root, yadah. A noun from this root is the term for Jew, yehudah. So when you say Jew or Judah you are enunciating the Hebrew word for thanks. Hence, we may say that to be a Jew one must be a grateful person. Thank-you in Hebrew is Todah.

Ram in Hebrew is yovel, a synonym of the familiar shofar, which means ram's horn. When an important milestone took place the ram's horn, also called yovel, was sounded. This forms the origin of the English words, jubilee, jubilate and jubilant.

Beloved in Hebrew is david. So when you call your friend David you are talking pure Hebrew. A cognate word is dod, which means uncle. Another form of the word is dodee, a female person you cherish. You say that word in the Sabbath hymn, L'chah Dodee, Come, My Beloved.

Ox in Hebrew is elef, which is what our ancestors were trying to depict when they designed the first letter of the language, the aleph (from which we get the word, alphabet, the second letter, beth, was a pictograph of a house). So when you say alphabet, you are really saying, "Ox house."

Twin in Hebrew is t'ome, the basis for the popular name, Thomas.

Heal in Hebrew is rafah, basis for the popular name, Raphael. Doctor in Hebrew is rofeh.

Stalk in Hebrew is kaneh, which yields us the English words, cane and canoe.

Judge in Hebrew is dan, origin of the name Daniel (the syllable, el, in so many of our names stands, of course, for God).

Life in Hebrew, as almost everyone knows, is chayim, a word which, like shalom, peace, has virtually been incorporated into the English language.

This is a tiny sampling of the plenitude of Hebrew words found in the names and terms regularly articulated in this land of ours. For other instances see your nearest rabbi, Hebrew teacher or Hebraist.

Zionism

Attacked by goons and buffoons, Zionism should be properly understood.

Zionism is not a movement to transfer the Jews of the world to Israel.

Zionism is the belief that those Jews who want a nation of their own should have a right to do so.

Zionism is not something confined to Jews. Anyone who believes in the right of a people to its own destiny is a Zionist.

Zionism can also be read as American-style democracy. The Arab leaders mistreat their own people and keep them in degradation, squalor and disease. They allow them no right to vote or to move up in the quality of living.

Zionism is the reverse of all that. It brings to the Israelis (including the Arabs and Christians there) freedom, the right to vote, good pay, good health and good education.

The effort to make a distinction between Jews and Zionists is a sneaky one. True, not every Jew is a Zionist, but when the anti-Semites (including Arab and Communist leaders) say they are opposed to Zionism but not Judaism, they are using the same tactic that other anti-Semites have used in declaring that they like "good" Jews but not the other kind.

Actually, the chief beneficiary of Zionism will ultimately be the Arab masses who will benefit from the modern trends being introduced into the Mideast by Jews.

The Bible

Ladies and Gentlemen, as a public service, we bring you a program devoted to an explanation of the Bible. Appearing on our program is a rabbi and an interviewer.

Rabbi: I am most appreciative of the invitation to take part in this program designed to give the general public a better understanding of modern religious thought. Today we will have a look at the Bible; for some of you, it may be a new look. Certainly, Holy Writ is worth examining and re-examining many times, and I hope that our discussion will stimulate you to acquire greater familiarity with Scriptures, and I hope you will derive greater usefulness from it, in accordance with the interpretation of your own particular faith.

Interviewer: I will ask questions that are often heard about the Bible as our way of evoking replies which can best illuminate this fascinating and oftimes complicated subject. I have often heard people ask the question, "Just what is the Bible; is it really a book?"

Rabbi: A fine question. Surprisingly enough, the answer is no. That is to say, that although the Bible looks like a book, and the material in the Bible has been put between covers, actually the Bible is really a collection of documents. As you know, the Bible contains many segments which are themselves called Books, like the Book of Samuel, the Book of Ruth, the Book of Kings, etc.

Interviewer: How many different books are there in the Bible?

Rabbi: In the Jewish Bible, known as the Old Testament, which is the Bible we'll talk about today, there are 39 books.

Interviewer: And are all the books of the Bible history and laws?

Rabbi: No. The amazing thing about the Bible is the variety of its subject matter. Some of the books are indeed chronicles, and two of the 39 books are called Chronicles. Other books contain primarily rules for living, such as the Book of Deuteronomy. Some of the books contain the sermons delivered by the greatest minds of antiquity, the prophets. Some books, such as Ecclesiastes and Job, contain philosophy. The Book of Proverbs, as the name indicates, contains wise sayings.

Interviewer: And, as I recall, some of the books are very pleasant stories.

Rabbi: True enough. The Book of Ruth is a fine story, as are Daniel and Esther and others.

Interviewer: And how would you classify the Book of Psalms? They're prayers, aren't they?

Rabbi: It is almost impossible to classify the Book of Psalms, because there is hardly anything like them in all literature. Yes, they are prayers, but they are prayers that once were sung. We would call them hymns today. They express the effort of the gifted sweet singers of Israel to attain communion with God in times of anguish and joy. They have been called the Jews' love letters to God. The Hebrew term for Psalms is tehillah, which is a word meaning praise, or adulation, and the Psalms do indeed exhibit not only the way the Jew prayed to God but praised Him. The most celebrated word in the Psalms, a Hebrew word which has become part of the English language, hallelujah, is a word related to the Hebrew word, tehilla, and it is translated, Praise ye the Lord.

Interviewer: Have we described all the contents of the Bible?

Rabbi: Not quite. The Bible contains what we might today call allegories, such as the Book of Daniel. It contains quite a lot of poetry, such as the famous songs of Deborah, Miriam, Moses, etc. And one book of the Bible is in a class by itself. It is a prolonged, poetic outcry to God. It is the Book of Lamentations, written to memorialize the temple when it was destroyed by the Babylonians. The poem is attributed to Jeremiah, the most poignant of the prophets.

Interviewer: Were all of these books written at the same time?

Rabbi: They were not. The Bible is an anthology, a collection of works written over a long period of time.

Interviewer: How long?

Rabbi: Some scholars say the time covered is about 1500 years.

Interviewer: How would you compare the Old Testament and the New Testament?

Rabbi: Well, it is not for me to venture a qualitative comparison. We in the Jewish faith maintain that the sentiments contained in the New Testament mostly duplicate the Old. But there is one objective set of comparisons on which we can all agree. Obviously, the New Testament is a smaller book. Also the New

Testament centers about one life, that of Jesus, containing as it does four accounts of his life, the Gospels, followed by the various letters, or Epistles of St. Paul. So the New Testament is a more condensed set of books than the Old, which does not feature any one individual, but records instead the history and teachings of an entire people over many centuries of time.

Interviewer: Who wrote the Bible?

Rabbi: Here again there is disagreement. In order to answer your question and help you the better to remember the contents of the Bible, let me explain the divisions of the Bible.

Interviewer: How many divisions are there?

Rabbi: There are 3 principal divisions. One includes the First Five Books. These are given especially sacred status in Jewish tradition. The First Five Books are ascribed to Moses himself. They record the events from the time of Creation to the death of Moses. The names of the First Five Books are familiar to most people. Some of the titles, by the way, come from the Greek and Latin and might be explained.

Interviewer: The First Book is Genesis, and that means Beginning - doesn't it?

Rabbi: Indeed it does. It traces history down to the death of Joseph. Then, the next book has a title which is not Greek, but Latin, although the word has been absorbed into the English language. It is Exodus, which, of course, refers to the departure of the Jews from Egypt. The Third Book deals primarily with the duties of the ancient Hebrew priests, and the name, Leviticus, means priestly. Surprisingly, however, this book which contains so many drab details about sacrifices, etc., soars to the greatest heights of sublimity.

Interviewer: What do you mean?

Rabbi: Well, right in the middle of the book, we read the glorious utterance, "Love thy neighbor as thyself," and the same chapter, Leviticus 19, also contains such gems as: "Do not take vengeance and do not bear a grudge." It also points out the necessity of loving the stranger.

Interviewer: How do you account for the fact that a book which is so humdrum reaches such spiritual heights?

Rabbi: I suppose it means to say that when we go about our daily lives we must lift ourselves up to noble behavior. The time to use your religion is when you're at work. The teachings of faith apply not only when we are in a place of religious meditation but when we are in the thick of mundane activities. The Fourth Book is known to us as the Book of Numbers because it begins with a census; it describes the wanderings of the Israelites in the desert and the instruction which Moses gave to them.

Interviewer: And the Fifth is Deuteronomy...

Rabbi: Yes, which is a Greek word meaning Repetition. Here Moses retells the story of the Israelites to the second generation of the desert, just before their entrance into the Holy Land. It is a superb book, Deuteronomy, with ideas which mankind has not yet attained. There is not time to list them all, but the book is eminently worth reading. Here, justice and fairness are described as the duties of mankind. Another obligation is to help the downtrodden and under-privileged. Compassion and commiseration, kindliness and mercy are called for, and a vision of the better society is constantly delineated. Now these first five books are known in the Hebrew tradition by the letter T.

Interviewer: The letter T?

Rabbi: T stands for Torah.

Interviewer: Just what does Torah mean?

Rabbi: The full explanation of that term is most complex. It is usually translated Law, but that is not quite accurate. For our purposes, let us say that the Hebrew word, Torah, means teaching and instruction. These five books are, as I said, given special sanctity in our faith. They are written on parchment and the Scroll itself, always kept in the Ark in the synagogue, is also called the Torah. The full term is Torat Moshe, the Instruction of Moses. The books are regarded as dictated by the Lord himself, and they are indeed worth being prized by all humanity. The books have been referred to as the Magna Carta which liberated mankind from paganism and from brutalitarianism. The books establish the idea of monotheism, the sacredness of every individual because of the spark of divinity within him, the great inspiration which we receive from such spiritual giants as Abraham, Isaac, Jacob and Moses, and it is therefore no wonder that these books are venerated by three great Western religions and are indeed revered by all men who bother to read them.

Interviewer: And what is the next section of the Bible?

Rabbi: The next section we call N.

Interviewer: Why is that?

Rabbi: The letter, N, is the first letter of the Hebrew word, N'vee-eem.

Interviewer: Which means what?

Rabbi: Which means prophets. According to Judaism, the gift of prophecy began with the Judges and reached its greatest heights with such mighty seers as Isaiah, Jeremiah, and Ezekiel.

Interviewer: Which books are listed as Prophets?

Rabbi: The so-called N section is divided into the early N's, the early prophets and the late ones. The books of the early prophets include Joshua, Judges, the two Books of Samuel and the two Books of Kings and then we have the later prophets, the three I mentioned, of whose works we have large portions, Isaiah, Jeremiah, and Ezekiel and twelve more, of whose writings we have smaller remnants: Amos, Hosea, Micah, Joel, Jonah, Nahum, Zephaniah, Zechariah, Obadiah, Habakkuk, Haggai, and Malachi.

Interviewer: Tell us something about the prophets.

Rabbi: Time does not allow a full explanation. Suffice it to say that the most exalted ideals which man is capable of capturing are contained in the prophetic writings, ideas we are still feebly trying to put into effect, such as world unity and world peace. No nation on earth could go awry if it attempted to follow the ideas of the prophets. They were the spokesmen of nobility and the fearless enunciators of sentiments as lofty as those which have ever been inspired by Almighty God.

Interviewer: And the word, prophet, means foreseer of the future?

Rabbi: No, that is a misconception. The word, prophet, does not mean, forecaster at all, although many believe that. The word, prophet, is misunderstood because the prefix, pro, has two meanings. The phet in the word, prophet, comes from the Greek word, to speak. And the prophets were indeed speakers, spokesmen, lecturers, preachers par excellence. The prefix, pro, has two meanings, one is in advance, as in prologue, or prognosticate. The other meaning of that little prefix is on behalf of, as in pro and con, in protagonist or pronoun. The prophets did not claim to be foreseers but they did speak for God. They were His champions. They did not possess clairvoyance, but they did understand what the consequences of injustice and unrighteousness would be. Because they were so often right in diagnosing the evils of their time they were thought to have the ability to predict the future, but they had no more ability in that regard than a mother when she says to a child, if you play with fire you will be burned. Such a child, if burnt, would misunderstand the purpose of the mother if it were to say, "Look, mommy is a fortuneteller!" What the mother was concerned about was not demonstrating her ability to anticipate what is coming but the behavior of her child. So it was with the prophets; they spoke in behalf of God and His Moral Law; they were not exhibiting any supernatural ability to foretell future events.

Interviewer: And what about the third division of the Bible?

Rabbi: The third segment contains a cluster of diverse books, some poetic, some historic, some philosophical, some lyrical, such as the Song of Songs, the variegated thoughts and fancies of a host of creative writers, all of them concerned with man's welfare and his relationship to God. These books constitute the third division of the Bible, called by the title of Writings, or to use the Hebrew, K'tubeem. We refer to them as K or Ch, pronounced gutturally. This section includes the Wisdom Books of Psalms and Proverbs and Ecclesiastes. The stories of Job, Daniel, Ruth and Esther, and the poetical books, Song of Songs and Lamentations, and the historical books of Ezra, Nehemiah, and two Books of Chronicles. Now, we take these three initials, T, N, and Ch, and we pronounce them as one word, Tanach, and that is the Hebrew designation of the Bible.

Interviewer: What can you tell us about these writings?

Rabbi: Every single one of them could occupy a full program. They contain the most profound and the most exalted of ideas. Unfortunately, our time does not allow us to elaborate on any of them, which might be just as well, since perhaps the mere mention of these books will stimulate some of our listeners to read or re-read them. Nothing you can do will be more profitable. If you want to read them for their full literary flavor, you might try the New Jewish Publication Society translations or the American Translations which attempts to render the Bible in the language which we use in this country and hence makes many of the passages much more intelligible.

Interviewer: In what style are most of our Bibles written?

Rabbi: Most of our Bibles, Jewish, Protestant and Catholic favor the Elizabethan type of English, which is not too comprehensible to us today.

Interviewer: And what about the new Revised Version of the Bible?

Rabbi: The newly authorized version prepared by the Protestant Church council utilizes more modern language in its translations. It is notable that that great masterpiece was accomplished with the aid of a great Jewish scholar, Dr. Harry Orlinsky, of the Hebrew Union College-Jewish Institute of Religion. Dr. Orlinsky is the editor of the New Jewish Translation. We now also have a Catholic Bible in modern parlance, it is The New American Bible.

Interviewer: Have the Dead Sea Scrolls produced any helpful new light for the better understanding of the Bible?

Rabbi: Strangely, they have not, although we would have to devote an entire program to this subject in order to explain my brief answer fully. Indeed, we have to terminate our discussion now, and we have scarcely gotten into the contents of the Bible.

Interviewer: Before we finish, could you tell me whether in your opinion the Bible is true?

Rabbi: That's too generalized a question, but I will say that much that we think is exaggerated has much truth in it. For instance, there may be debate as to whether or not the Noah story actually happened, but can anyone challenge what the story tells us, namely, that if human beings are going to be corrupt, the world will be destroyed? The latest discovery of science, the atomic bomb, has validated one of the most ancient stories of mankind, the story of the Flood. There is much more of value in the Bible if only we understand it properly, with the guidance of spiritual leaders. It will not take long to convince you that even though every section of the Bible is not as sacred as every other one, there is much in Scriptures that is of helpfulness to mankind today. The Bible is old, but is far from old-fashioned; it is ancient, but it is not antiquated; it is venerable, but it is far from dated. Its truths can greatly help us if only we would read and heed. And the more we would study the Bible the more convincing would become that statement in Proverbs; "The beginning of wisdom is the fear of the Lord" May all of you derive information and inspiration from each exposure to Holy Writ and may you better understand the requirements of the Lord as you re-read the utterances of those who have been touched by the spirit of the Lord.

The Book of Job

The greatest literary achievement of all times is said to be the Book of Job.

Found in the Jewish Bible, Job is the well known story about the righteous man who undergoes horrible suffering.

The question raised by the book is, "Why do the innocent suffer?"

The book is literarily superb. Translated all over again by the great scholar, Rabbi Robert Gordis, the poem contains passages of sublimity. Especially touching is the list of virtues which Job enumerates: kindliness, considerateness, gentleness, charitableness, devotion to family. It is a compendium of those qualities glorified in Judaism (even though Job is not necessarily delineated as being Jewish).

What makes Job both timely and timeless is the message that we are wrong in thinking that our woes are necessarily the consequences of our own conduct.

When something bad happens to us we are prone to cry, "What did I do to deserve this?"

True, some things we do will result in suffering. If you desecrate your body through excessive smoking, sleeplessness, or the taking of alcohol or other drugs, you are certainly going to suffer. But a lot of things happen to us that are not the result of our wickedness but the result of the wickedness or the carelessness of others. Therefore, we must not feel the sense of guilt whenever a reversal or adversity strikes.

Much of the Bible lays down a connection between our actions and what happens to us. The Book of Job is great because it seeks to change that connection. We should love God, says the author of Job, because of the general benefits He bestows upon us, not because we have been shielded from harm. Like a parent, God seeks our good. If we deviate from prudent behavior or are caught up by circumstances beyond our control that does not mean that divine love does not hold sway for us.

So the Book of Job has a important message for us today. It is our task to reduce as mush a possible those social situations which make for problems.

To live up to the message of Job is quite a job.

Alice in Bibleland

Alice(Walks on stage, accompanied by some kind of 4-
legged creature, unless that is too difficult to stage):

Hello, I send you
My greeting,
Mind if I join you
At this meeting?

You remember me
I pray and I hope,
If you never heard of me,
You must be a dope.

I'm Alice, the girl of
Wonderland fame,
If you haven't read about me,
What a terrible shame!

I'm breaking in
On your party today,
Because I want to
Take you on my way.

I'm not the president;
I don't have the gavel,
However, please join me,
As we begin to travel.

Where are we going?
Through a land of wonder,
I mean our Bible, unless
we blunder.

We won't do all of it,
We'll do a little trimmin',
We'll meet on the way,
Some very famous women.

We'll meet some ladies
Of worth and jollity,
For, you know, in the Bible
There is female equality.

(Hears one approaching. Puts ear to hand)

Let's see, I hear
Someone coming,
And don't I also hear
Someone drumming.

(Enter Deborah, the Judge, dressed perhaps in a kind
of judicial outfit worn in a nomadic country, whatever
that would be like.)

An Attendant:
Hear ye, hear ye,
Stand still, don't budge,
Make way for her honor,
Deborah the Judge.

Alice:
A woman judge,
Isn't that nice,
I bow to you, Deborah,
In fact I'll bow twice.

Deborah:
You need not bow, my child,
And you certainly are a beauty,
No one has to bow to me
In my line of duty.

We judges only ask one thing,
That people be decent,

This is true in our day,
And in your time more recent.

We Jews are proud that
We gave the world a gift;
The idea of fairness and justice,
From which we must not shift.

We must be nice to one another
To avoid God's fury,
That applies to each of us,
And also to each jury.

(Holds up sign. One says J-U-R-Y.
The other J-E-W-R-Y)

Alice;
What an honor
To meet her honor
She has so much
Dignity upon her.

Before the time of Deborah
There were also ladies of fame,
I wonder whether I can remember
Every heroine's name.

Let's see. Abraham had a wife,
Or did he have a pair-a?
Oh I remember now,
Her name was Sarah.

(Enter Sarah, in outfit like a princess)

And Isaac had a lovely wife,
Of whom our Scriptures tell.

Her name was Rebecca,
And she's famous for her well.

(Out comes Rebecca, in shepherdess costume, carrying a pitcher)

And Isaac's son Jacob
Married Rachel who was so sweet,
To get her, he worked seven years
And seven more in tropical heat.

(Enter Rachel, with a kind of a Syrian outfit. with lots of color)

These are the heroines
Of the Torahs in our Arks,
Welcome to our happy midst,
O lovely matriarchs.

Sarah;
We are pleased to know you.

Rebecca:
You, daughters and you, mothers.

Rachel:
We hope you're always kind.

Sarah:
To your husbands and your brothers.

Rebecca:
We hope you live according.

Rachel:
To shining Jewish ideals.

Sarah:
And that the religion we created.

Rebecca:
To all of you still appeals.

Sarah, Rebecca, Rachel:
Our husbands brought to this earth
A way of acting and living,
Which makes men feel so good,
When they're serving and they're giving.

(Step aside)

Alice:
O three Matriarchs, thanks,
You stimulate the mind,
You also stir the heart
And remind us to be kind.

(Enter Miriam. She is also something of a shepherdess, with a crook, perhaps, but maybe with something
which suggests the long journey through the desert.)

Miriam:
Forty years of wandering
Is no bed of roses,
But it was worth it,
To be so close to Moses.

I am his sister,
And that makes me proud
We tried to understand God
In the fire and cloud.

Moses taught us
That God could be seen
When we are helpful
Instead of mean.

Moses taught us
That God can be seen
When we control ourselves
And are morally clean.

Moses taught us
That God can be seen
When love in a family
Remains strong and keen.

Alice:
Thank you, Miriam
For what you have taught
You're like Moses
In grandeur of thought.

You see how many ladies
Play important parts
Both in the Bible
And in our hearts.

There was another
Who sought the truth,
And found it in Judaism,
Her name was Ruth.

(Enter Ruth)

Ruth:
Yes, I became Jewish
Voluntarily, you see.

I became Jewish
Because I wanted to be.

I loved Jewish ideas
And Jewish ways;
The prayers are beautiful
And the holidays.

Every religion is pleasant
And probably heaven-sent,
I chose the Jewish one,
And much to me it meant.

Alice:
Yes, Ruth, we know
You are a famous one
Because of your choice and King David,
Your celebrated grandson.

There's another Bible heroine
With whom we're all acquainted,
So brave that in another faith
She certainly would be sainted.
She scaled the heights and

She scaled the heights
And occupied a throne,
But she never got too high
To hear her people groan.

(Exit Ruth)

She was a queen;
When her people got in a jam,
She fought back with courage,
She was no Persian lamb.

(Enter Esther in full regalia)

Esther;
I heard your compliment
And thank you very much,
It's terrible to get so mighty
That you lose the common touch.

A book in the Bible
Is named after me,
But my greatest joy
Was to see my people free.

O daughters of Israel,
Living after the Bible time,
Remember that cowardice
Is the greatest crime.

Stand up for good things,
Have the courage to love
And good things will come to
You, from up above.

Come, my sisters,
Of Bibleland
Let us take
Each other's hand.

(They join hands)

Bible Heroines Ensemble:
We want to give you
Something to cherish,
It is a thought
That will never perish.

Mothers and girls,
More precious than jewels
Is the wisdom which
You learn in schools.

More beautiful
Than gorgeous dresses,
Is family love
Which warms and blesses.

Hold on to these,
And your voyage through life,
Will contain less heartache,
Much less strife.

You will find that life
Takes on extra flavor
If you help a friend,
Or do a favor.

And now farewell,
Until next we call
And may the good Lord
Bless you all.

(Exeunt)

How can we prove there is a God?

We can't.

The existence of God is a hypothesis, that is an assumption, but one which rests on logic.

If it is doesn't rest on logic, we are not asked in Judaism to accept it.

But think for a moment. Everything in the world reflects a maker and a purpose. Shall we say that the only thing in the world without a maker and a purpose is the world itself?

Because we cannot behold God does not mean that He does not exist. We cannot see electricity, yet we know there is such an entity, for we use it. We cannot see intelligence, yet we measure it.

We know there is electricity and intelligence because we see their results.

So we think we see the results of God's work: in nature, in human nature, and in the orderly symmetry of the universe. Look through a telescope and you see system; look through a microscope, and you see system. The author of these intricate systems, as well as of life itself, with all of its complexities, we call God.

Some Jewish philosophers have said that God laid down certain rules which He will not transgress. For example, He will not make tomorrow yesterday or make two and two equal five. To us the greatest miracle is not the stoppage of nature, but the regular process of life.

God also, according to a point of view held by some Jewish thinkers, limits himself in another way. He will not force you and me to believe in Him or to accept His commandments.

He wants us to be good. He wants mankind to be peaceful. But He does not treat us as though we were puppets. He lets us know what is right, and the way that we discover what is right is through our conscience (which is fortified by religious teachings) is also something of a miracle. But then He permits us to choose whether we, or society, will obey Him.

This is called Freedom of Will, and implies that mankind must **decide** to walk the path leading to equality and justice, brotherhood and harmony. This means that Judaism does not accept such ideas as predestination or determinism. You might look up these words in the dictionary.

Judaism contends that God is good, and that evil comes to the world when we disregard the instructions we get from Him.

Of course, the Jewish idea of God is that He is invisible, of a form that is beyond our imagining, and that He is absolutely One, not zero, not two, not three, but One.

Religion and Science

Wasn't it interesting that the Book of Genesis received such nice "publicity" during the moon shots?

Those intrepid astronauts were trying to tell the world that science and religion are not at odds; they are partners.

The more we learn about the universe the more we have reason to marvel at the "Brain" that concocted it all.

Some people who absorb a little science are inclined to react to the Bible with "Aw!". Others, like the moon-men, react with "awe."

Could the symmetries of the cosmos, so reliable that you can thrust an object thousands of miles into space and know that you can count on certain laws to work, be the product of chance?

So it was fitting that the heroes of space should pay tribute to the Creator and to Genesis, the story which tells us that the world, despite its diversities, is one.

Some there are who cavil at the space program. They say it is true "lunacy" to make lunar shots when money is needed to cure cancer and misery in the world.

Perhaps a by-product of the space exploration program will be the rediscovery of the truth of the statements in the Bible that the world is one and, if men will live up to the mandate of the Bible, humanity can also become one.

The author, holding the Scroll, as his son, Barry, makes out the unvocalized Hebrew in preparation for his Bar Mitzvah.

Reform Judaism Examined

Tell me something about Reformed Judaism...

Did I hear you say Reformed?

Yes, is that wrong?

We do not refer to it as Reformed, but as Reform.

Why?

Because Reformed implies that we have arrived at a certain place and are going to remain there, but Reform means reforming, that the process of change is continuing.

The process of change. Is that the characteristic of Reform?

There are many characteristics of Reform. As for making changes, we have changed the attitude towards change.

I don't follow.

Let me try to explain. One thing that has always marked Judaism is its ability to adapt itself to new circumstances by making adjustments.

You mean, by adopting new ideas?

Not necessarily. The remarkable thing about Judaism is that it always held on fast to its basic ideas.

What are they?

Well, for one, that the world is a unit...

What is the significance of that idea?

It's quite significant. If you accept the idea that the world is a unit, you feel a new horror towards hatred and hostility, because then every conflict becomes a civil war.

And there's nothing civil about a civil war.

Right. And if you accept the idea that the world is a unit you more easily see that the author of the world is Himself One and One who transcends the work of His hands. Here you find the key to the unique Jewish idea of God's oneness. We don't believe that the world was created accidentally and that therefore there is no God. We don't believe that the universe is split into two forces, one good and one evil. We believe rather that the evil and tragedy of life represent incompleteness which God and man in partnership must remedy. Nor do we subscribe to any splitting up of godliness into three or any other number. And if you accept the belief in God's unity, it must follow that all of the world's people represent one family, each one containing a bit of godliness and therefore so precious that we must not harm nor hurt one another. Because the person who is poor or oppressed is your brother, you must share what you have with him. This is what motivated Joseph in the Bible, and is the ground principle for the practice of charity among Jews. This explains why Judaism provided the genesis of democracy, of mutual aid societies, of efforts for peace, of educational programs designed to fill up the mind with knowledge that will prompt the heart to obey the teachings of the Lord.

All this comes from Reform Judaism?

No, all this is fundamental Judaism.

And how does Reform Judaism enter the picture?

Well, these principles were symbolized through a number of practices in ancient times.

And then what?

Well, the practices changed from era to era. The need for giving up some of your means for good causes was formerly illustrated by the system of animal sacrifices. But Judaism outgrew this custom, and other illustrative rituals were adopted. The process of change was deliberately advanced in each generation.

Beginning with the time of the Bible?

Yes, the Bible itself represents many changes, from primitive ideas to sublime ideals. It was written over a period of 1500 years. Then, afterwards as new situations arose, the sages adjusted the teachings of the Bible to their times.

You mean another Bible was written?

Well, not quite another Bible. Commentaries on the Bible were produced, bringing the Biblical regulations up to date. One set of commentaries was called the Mishnah, and the addenda to the Mishnah were called the Gemara, and both of them together are known as the Talmud.

This sounds like what happened in the United States. The law was the Constitution, then new laws, based on the Constitution, were written.

Right you are. The Bible could be called the Jewish Constitution and the Talmud might be compared to the laws which have flowed from the Constitution. Some of these laws deal with matters completely undreamed of by our founding fathers but they adhere to the principles of the Constitution. This is the process which Reform Judaism stresses.

And where was Reform Judaism during the days of the Bible and the Talmud?

Where was your face before it was washed this morning?

I don't quite understand.

I'll try to clarify. As I have said, this process of fluidity and change always marked Judaism. Then in the 16th century, a rabbi named Joseph Karo collected the majority decisions of the Talmudic rabbis and set them down in a book.

What was his purpose?

His purpose was merely to make a record of what the sages had agreed on. But his book known as the Set Table (Hebrew: Shulchan Aruch) was lifted to a new dimension by others.

What do you mean by that?

Karo had meant to list the practices that were the last word. But others began to regard his book as though it were the final word. The result was the slow-down of the process of interpretation, modification and elaboration. Something new had entered Judaism, the freezing of its forms. This is what today we call Orthodoxy, one of the most drastic reforms that Judaism ever underwent.

And how long did this continue?

For about 250 years, until in the early 1800's a group of laymen in Germany realized that Judaism had become a faith that was difficult to practice except in an all-Jewish environment.

And by that time Jews were living in a freer world.

Yes, Napoleon is credited with having opened up the ghettos. His regime helped to liberate the Jews physically, but religiously they were still hamstrung by a host of customs and practices which prevented them from functioning in society at large. And it is imperative for Jews to mingle with other people.

Why do you say that?

Because it is another one of the cardinal principles of Judaism that it must impart its ideals to the world. Judaism is a failure unless it brings a message of holiness to society. Now, if we are to be cut and shut off from the world by self-imposed restrictions, we cannot fulfill our assignment.

So what happened?

What happened was that a group of laymen revised the Orthodox worship practices and boldly made changes in Jewish ritual and customs comparable to those that had been made in Biblical and Talmudical times. The most notable of the laymen who pioneered in these measures was Israel Jacobson, who, at great cost to himself financially and in terms of popularity, sponsored a synagogue and introduced so many changes in Jewish forms that the movement he started is called Reform Judaism.

And what do you think the name implies?

The name is significant. Jacobson and the rabbis who followed him did not want a new religion, nor did they want new principles. All they sought to do was to reform Judaism, alter its outward appearance so that the baic ideals could be released for fresher and more effective functioning. Soon the movement spread to America.

When did Reform reach America?

Shortly after the Jacobson moves were made in Germany, stirrings towards Reform were made in the U.S., the first place being in the Sephardic synagogue in Charleston, S.C.

What happened in Charleston?

It was havoc for a while. A group asked for the modernization of the worship and the abandonment of some customs. The request was indignantly rejected. Two factions grew up. Ultimately, however, the Charleston temple became Reform. Others followed suit, especially when there came to these shores a number of brilliant rabbis devoted to the refashioning of Judaism so that it would better harmonize with the free atmosphere of this democracy. Most resonant voice for Reform in America was Dr. David Einhorn, of Baltimore.

Wasn't there a Rabbi Wise?

Right you are. An immigrant from Bohemia who came here in 1846 was Rabbi Isaac Mayer Wise who became the founder of the major institutions of Reform

Judaism, which still flourish today. He brought system and organization into Jewish life. He founded the first school in this country for the training of rabbis, the Hebrew Union College which later merged with another rabbinical school, the Jewish Institute of Religion, founded by another Rabbi Wise, Dr. Stephen S. Wise. Isaac founded the first association of rabbis, the Central Conference of American Rabbis. Not only is American Reform Judaism indebted to his organizing genius, but so are the other Jewish denominations, for what he pioneered in, they imitated. Even his changes were adopted by many so-called traditionalist groups.

What then are the earmarks of Reform Judaism?

Well, first of all, a return to the classical fluidity of forms in order to make the principles operable in every kind of environment.

And next?

Next we might list the fact that Reform abandoned a lot of notions which Judaism had acquired from its European neighbors.

Such as?

Such as superstitions, and excessively mystical notions, and most practices associated with "the evil spirits." These were tossed out, or, at least, re-interpreted.

What about the wearing of the hat?

The hat at worship, like the ban on music at worship, is in the category of trivialities which had been magnified far out of their original significance. Hats were not worn in Biblical days. Later, hats were worn at worship. The putting on of the hat was a reform introduced into Judaism in order to conform to the prevailing manner of showing respect. Well, in our part of the world men show respect by removing the hat; hence we do at worship. But if you want to wear a hat in a Reform temple, go ahead, it doesn't make that much difference.

What about the playing of musical instruments in the temple?

This is part of another change brought about by Reform. Because Jews had suffered so intensely they longed for release from their agony in the form of a deliverer or a Messiah. They were told that they were expelled from their Holy Land because of their misdeeds and they must remain in a posture of mourning until the miraculous restoration of the temple and its sacrificial system by the Messiah. Hence no instrumental music.

What did Reform do with the concept?

Well, Reform didn't minimize the tragedy of the destruction of Palestine and the Temple, but Reform asserted that it was un-Jewish to concentrate entirely on the past and to declare that forever afterwards the chief function of Judaism was to wait until that past was restored. So we pointed out that Judaism was a religion of optimism and of hope for the future. Hence, we will manifest joy in the synagogue as they used to in the temple of old and play musical instruments if we want. We also changed the outlook towards the dietary laws.

Have you repealed them?

Reform says that they are not obligatory. Like other practices, if they are to be observed, it is not because we have to do them but because we want to do them as voluntary acts of love for God and for His teaching.

So Reform has been pretty negative, eh?

That has often been said, but it is not so. We deleted prayers dealing with the personal Messiah. That is so. We discarded other passages which expressed superstitious ideas to which we no longer subscribed. That is so. We abandoned other things which we felt we had outgrown or which have no meaning for us. But we wrote many prayers of our own. We created new customs such as Confirmation and Consecration and the Congregational Seder and Family Worship. We added to Judaism the auxiliaries of each temple. We restored to Judaism the equality of women in religious matters. We created a teenage movement. We devised new methods of religious education and developed a fine library of Jewish textbooks for young and old alike. We reintroduced the sermon into the worship. We are not negative. In fact, Reform "innovated" the late Friday night service, now in vogue among Orthodox and Conservative synagogues.

And Is the Reform movement growing?

It certainly is. Remember what I said before, though. The true measure of the impact of Reform is not only the size of the Reform movement but also the tremendous influence it has had upon its sister denominations. American Orthodoxy reflects many Reform approaches and in many ways Conservatism is a copy of Reform. As for our own movement, in recent years the number of Reform temples in America has doubled and the membership in Reform has tripled. Today the Union of American Hebrew Congregations is a network of over 700 temples comprising a membership of over one and a half million people.

And what is Reform's attitude towards Zionism?

Early Reformers were afraid of Zionism. They thought it clashed with their theological notions about the right of the Jew to live in the world at large. Later, it was realized that if Reform declares that Jews have a right to live anywhere, one of the places they ought to be allowed to live in is Palestine. Hence, it has been officially declared that there is no conflict between the advocacy of Reform and the advocacy of Zionism. But today Zionism is hardly a matter of debate.

And has Reform Judaism yet to come to the State of Israel?

In some measure. There are about ten Reform congregations there and a branch of the Reform Jewish Seminary. The people of Israel are ideally attuned to the principles of Reform. Both Reform Jews and Israeli Jews are possessed of the mission idea, the belief that it is the destiny of the Jews to widen the area of kindliness in human affairs. Both Reform Jews and Israeli Jews are amenable to experimentation with methods which will bring new avenues for Jewish creativity. At the present, however, Israel is so beset by economic and military troubles that it is wrong to press for her religious reforms. You remember how it was when our own American nation was begun. It was ringed by enemies who sought to crush it and it was quite a while before we were stabilized. But when greater stability comes, Reform will flourish in Israel. Those of its people who know about it desire it.

So how, then, do you summarize the characteristics of Reform Judaism?

To us Reform Judaism is Judaism with maximum relevance to our times. It is a series of emphases. We emphasize the rational above the mystical. We emphasize the here and now over the uncertain future of an afterlife. We emphasize man's capacity for improvement. We emphasize the equality of women. We emphasize the joyful over the sorrowful, the optimistic over the desultory. We emphasize the partnership between God and man in the improvement of human welfare. We emphasize the prophetic above the liturgic, the spiritual over the ritual. We emphasize the free-will spirit of voluntary offerings to God over the obligatory. We emphasize the holiness which is to be created out of mundane experiences over the holiness to be found in removing ourselves from the actions and passions of society. We emphasize the fluid over the fixed in forms, even as we stress the eternality of the fundamental concepts known as Judaism. This is Reform Judaism.

And what is the relationship between Reform and the other Jewish denominations.?

We are getting along together fine. We believe not only in ecumenism with our Christian brethren, but also with our fellow-Jews. The differences between Reform and the more traditional groups are diminishing, as Reform considers the re-adoption of some ceremonies which it gave up before, as Conservatism and Orthodoxy move closer to the Reform position in some respects. Jews are moving closer to one another, and it has been predicted that in the United States one Jewish denomination may yet emerge, synthesizing and coalescing the existing three.

It is true that some Orthodox Jews still regard Reform as close to Christianity, but examination shows that Reform clings to the basic tenets of Judaism. On the other hand, there are some Reform Jews who look upon Orthodoxy as still medieval, but closer examination here shows that Orthodoxy and Conservatism have joined Reform in many ways in accentuating the best of the ancient and combining it with a modern cadence.

Thank you, and is everyone welcome to attend Jewish services?

Yes, and everyone is welcome to ask more questions. You can get the answers from your nearest rabbi.

The Pharisees

One of the greatest wrongs in history is the stigmatization of the Pharisees in the New Testament.

In numerous passages the Pharisees are branded and castigated so that in all succeeding generations the word, Pharisaic, has become a disagreeable term, even ending up in the dictionary as a synonym for hypocritical.

Is this characterization true?

It is not. It is absolutely not.

Why then is Jesus depicted as hurling insults at the Pharisees? Who were they and what were they really like?

One must remember that the New Testament is not only a book containing sublime sentiments and ideals. It is also something of a "campaign document," written to win the Roman world over to Christianity at a time when it and Judaism were vying for favor.

At the turn of the millennium, the Roman throne and people controlled the world. Whoever could win the fealty of the imperial family and city would religiously dominate society.

The rivalry at that time between the newly formed faith which came to be known as Christianity and its mother faith, Judaism, was keen.

The New Testament was partly "aimed" at the Roman world. It offered a new faith other than the paganism with which Romans were becoming disenchanted. But it had to "compete" with Judaism, then a missionary religion.

The Bishop and the Rabbi. Famed Archbishop Fulton J. Sheen after an appearance at a Sabbath eve service in Temple Sinai. The lady is Mrs. Silver, wife of the author.

Passages in the New Testament, then, were directed towards disparaging Judaism and glorifying Christianity. Part of the endeavor called for the "exculpation" of the Romans. One could hardly whitewash the Roman occupation force completely, especially the procurator, Pontius Pilate, one of the most savage men in history. But the effort is made in the pages of the New Testament, nonetheless, to play down Pontius' guilt and to play up the guilt of the Jews.

The spiritual leaders of the Jews at that period were the Talmudists. In the New Testament they are called Pharisees, a word whose etymology is uncertain. In Jewish sources they are seldom called Pharisees. They are known as "the sages," "the rabbis," the "teachers."

The New Testament, being of multiple authorship (like the Jewish Bible) has various things to say about the Pharisees. In some parts they are depicted favorably. St. Paul (originally named Saul) is described as a Pharisee and the disciple of one named Gamaliel. Jesus is at one point (Luke 11) seen fraternally dining with some members of the group. And one close follower of Jesus, Nicodemus, is described as a Pharisee.

But in other places unsparing words of condemnation are ascribed to Jesus vis-a-vis the Pharisees. How many millions of minds have been antisemitized by those statements, nay, how many Jewish martyrs have paid the cost for them -- these are incalculables.

What is the indictment against the Pharisees?

One, that they put the letter of the law above the spirit. Is this true? It is not. What especially typified their teaching was precisely their insistence that the Bible must be brought up to date, that it must be modified when new circumstances arose, that interpretation must be given latitude. In this respect they were opposed by the Sadduccees, another group, who were the "strict constructionists" of their day, whereas the Pharisees were the exponents of the "liberal" stance over against the literal.

One of the most famous examples of this stress on broadening the scope of Biblical law was the ruling of the Pharisees that the Scriptural reference to "an eye for an eye," meant that the criminal must pay "the equivalent of an eye" for the hurt he inflicted, which is the basis for modern laws of "damages." We must remember that the original Biblical assertion was a drastic modification of the rule that prevailed in ancient times, that a person had to give "a life" for an eye.

The Pharisees are charged with being hypocrites. Nothing could be further than the truth. In all history no more honest group of people ever lived. Their hundreds of maxims calling for honesty, sincerity, for the closing of the gap between preachment and practice, were carried out by these remarkable men in the way they lived.

The Pharisees are said to have been "legalistic." Untrue. The Pharisees concocted the so-called "oral" addenda to the Bible, and leaned over backwards to give people the benefit of the doubt. Anyone who glances into a translation of the Talmud will discover immediately how often the Pharisees opted on the side of mercy and compassion.

The Pharisees are painted as cruel and harsh. The opposite is the case. What makes the situation especially poignant is the fact that many of the ethical utterances attributed to Jesus are really Pharisaic. There is a book showing how the Sermon on the Mount derives directly from the teachings of the Pharisees. So Jesus himself, whilst delineated as being a foe of the Pharisees, is Pharisaic in many of his declarations and deeds. Indeed, he never ceased being a loyal Jew, i.e. Pharisaic.

Back in 1930, a Christian, Madison C. Peters, became so heart-broken by a wave of antisemitism which hit our nation, that he was moved to study Judaism and ultimately write a book called "Justice to the Jew."

After he completed the book, he found himself with a cluster of Pharisaic statements so beautiful that he decided to gather them together for another book which he called "Wit and Wisdom of the Talmud."

Among the entries in his book, Peters included these:

"He who gives way to his wrath makes desolate his house."

"Arrogance is a kingdom without a crown."

"Ignorance and conceit go hand in hand."

"Good deeds are better than creeds."

"Be in the habit of receiving every man with a pleasant countenance."

On and on go the Pharisaic dicta, sounding much like the sayings of Jesus, who was also influenced by the

Pharisees in the way he dramatized concepts through parables. No gentler man ever lived than one of the most illustrious of the Pharisees, Hillel, who said, among other things: "Do not unto others what you would not want them to do unto you."

In general, the Jews have obeyed Hillel's dictum and have not sought vengeance for the great harm done to them. That is why Israel Zangwill once said: "The people of Christ have become the Christ among peoples."

Many sensitive Christians, however, have sought to atone for the injury done to the Jews by the tendentious and polemical passages of the New Testament. The Roman Catholic Church in its celebrated Vatican Council statement made some amends to the Jews.

And many Christian scholars have helped in this effort. Books by R. Travers Herford, Frederick Grant, James Parkes, A. Roy Eckardt and others have patiently endeavored to set the record straight. It is Parkes who somewhere refers to "the New Testament travesty of the nature of Pharisaism."

An objective view will show us that the major teachings of Jesus and the Pharisees, like those of Judaism and Christianity, are remarkably similar. May the "lover's quarrel," as Bishop Fulton Sheen describes the tensions between Judaism and Christianity, come to a peaceful conclusion.

A Bedtime Prayer

I wanted to write a prayer for my youngsters to say at bedtime.

There are many such prayers.

Somehow none satisfied me.

So I produced one of my own.

After thinking and thinking, I came up with this beginning:

As I go to sleep tonight,
I pray to You with all my might,
Help me to be gay and bright,
Always be my parents' delight.

Then I was stymied. After much cogitation I came up with a tentative last line: "And teach me to do what's right."

But I gave that last line more thought. Teach me to do what's right!

Of course we should do what's right.

But often we do it because we have to, or because the policeman is watching us, or because we're ashamed to do differently.

To do what's right is commendable. But there must be a higher, more praiseworthy stage.

After many days, I came up with a last line I liked, and
so my amended, edited prayer goes like this:

As I go to sleep tonight,
I pray to You with all my might,
Help me to be gay and bright,
Always be my parents' delight,
And teach me to **enjoy** what's right.

Doing what's right is fine; enjoying what's right is true
maturity, for then we have attained the point where we
derive our pleasure from correct, proper conduct.
Everyone wants satisfaction. The test of a true person
is what gives him satisfaction. May ours come,
thrillingly and tinglingly and joyously, from doing
what is right, what will contribute to the fashioning of a
better, cleaner world, worthy of the presence in it of
the spirit of Almighty God.

Jewish Idea of Holiness

What is the Jewish concept of "holiness?"

The word is used very frequently. Like so many words from the religious lexicon it has even found its way into colloquialisms.

To many people something that is holy is something that is separated from the phenomena of normal living. A holy object must be treated with special veneration. It must be kept in a particular place. It must be handled gingerly. It must be displayed only on solemn occasions. It is somehow detached from our regular, day-to-day experiences.

So it is with the High Holydays. They are a period apart from the rest of the year, in the opinion of many. They represent a peak in the year. We ascend and then descend. During this season we deviate from our normal habitat, worshipping at length, and in general wrenching ourselves loose from our conventional regimen.

This extraordinary posture of what we think is piety is in keeping with a popular conception of what holiness implies.

It would be well, therefore, for us to discover, once and for all, that the idea of holiness outlined above is not a Jewish one.

In Judaism holiness is not measured by the degree to which you remove yourself from life. It is determined by what you do in the very thick of your daily life.

In Judaism sacred vessels are treated with respect, but not with awe. They are not objects invested with magical qualities, but they are mementos of what you must do every day if you are to impart a touch of meaningfulness to your existence.

Jewish Torahs are well-worn, and should be, for the Torah is not venerated as a mystical relic but is to serve as a guide for your course of activities every week. The Kiddush cup can be touched, handled, and fingered by all, for it has no other purpose but to remind you that, in the midst of commercial and domestic transactions, it is incumbent upon you to engender sweetness if you are to live up to God's expectations. The Shofar is a holy object in Judaism, not because it can produce some miracle but because it is a call to conscience, a call that you are supposed to heed not only in the synagogue but in the office, in the neighborhood where you live and in the home.

In short, in Judaism holiness is not something apart from life, but something which is a part of life. Judaism declares that holiness, which can be called the glow which comes from living in accordance with our higher capacities, is derived from the utilization of religious ideals and the constant embodiment of the meaning of religious symbols and rituals into the fabric of our normal actions and passions.

To illustrate the Jewish idea of holiness, let us take a few examples. Money would certainly not normally be regarded as a sacred item: it represents utter materialism and is a symbol of cupidity. But when you take some of your money and, denying yourself something you might yearn for, donate it to a good cause, you have achieved an act of holiness. Indeed, then the money itself is transformed from something secular into something sacred. You have made it holy by the use you have put it to. You have performed a sacrifice. And if you will look up the origin of the word, sacrifice, you will discover that it means to make sacred.

Holiness, therefore, in Judaism is not a quality; it is a process. Objects and acts are not endowed with an independent quality known as holiness; they become so by the nature of their usage.

The Pharisees, those badly maligned architects of the Jewish faith whom we designate as "the rabbis," have filled the Talmud with instances of how holiness can be achieved.

They have told us that lust, canalized and elevated through a decent family life, can be transformed into love.

They have told us that ambition, applied not only to the gratification of one's ego, but raised to the point where one is ambitious to serve others, can be lifted to the point of holiness.

They have told us that the human quest of joy can be hallowed so that we can ultimately derive as much delight from giving as we instinctively derive from getting.

They have told us that hatred, directed not at individuals but at evil, can be the source of much good.

They have told us that virtually any mundane phenomenon can be sanctified or hallowed, that it is indeed the objective of religion to transmute the material into the moral, the homely into the holy.

So, in our synagogues and in our homes let us, with renewed insight, understand what is expected of us if we are to live up to the criteria of holiness a la Judaism.

Frequently Asked
Questions about Judaism

Q. Is the "Old Testament" God harsh and cruel?

A. To some of those who wrote the earlier portions of the Jewish Bible, He seemed so. But gradually the Israelites improved their understanding and we see Old Testament passages in which the Almighty One is "long suffering" and full of compassion for His children. See, in the Ten Commandments, "showing mercy unto the thousandth generation" (Exodus 20.6). Remember, that the Jewish Bible was written over a span of 1500 years, and remember also, that the Bible was not written in the sequence with which it appears in its present form.

Q. Does the Old Testament declare that the sins of the fathers are visited upon the children?

A. Quite the contrary. See Ezekiel 18.20: "The son shall not bear the iniquity of the father, neither shall the father bear the iniquity of the son, the righteousness of the righteous shall be upon him, and the wickedness of the wicked shall be upon him."

Q. What are the names of the months in the Jewish calendar?

A. Beginning with Tishri (which is really the seventh month but which inaugurates the Spiritual New Year), we then proceed to: Cheshvan, Kislev, Tevet, Shvat, Adar (which is doubled on the Jewish leap year), Nisan (which is really the first month, when Spring begins and Passover occurs), Iyar, Sivan, Tamuz, Ab, and Elul.

Q Did the Jews crucify Jesus?

A. No. This delicate matter was treated most succintly by a scholar-rabbi, Dr. Theodore N. Lewis, of

Famous personages at Temple Sinai Services. In upper photo, Dr. Norman Vincent
Peale serves as guest preacher one Sabbath eve. Facing the congregation and
seated are the author and the former
mayor of Stamford, Bruno Giordano. In
lower right photo, Bishop Walter Curtis,
spiritual head of the Bridgeport Diocese, is
giving the Sabbath eve sermon. In both
lower photos the man on the extreme right
is the celebrated Roman Catholic priest,
Rev. George B. Ford.

Brooklyn, N.Y. thus: "The trial as described in the New Testament violates every principle of Jewish criminal law, which renders it utterly untenable from a Jewish point of view...The Jews literally could not demand that Pilate execute a fellow-Jew, and especially Pilate, the most detested of Roman procurators in Palestine, a beast in human form, whose savagery and corruption ultimately forced Rome to recall him. The truth is that the Gospels are theological books composed by men who were eager to shift responsibility for the crucifixion from Rome to the Jews in order to incur the favor of Roman rulers ...Crucifixion was not only unknown to Jewish law, but foreign to the Jewish concept of justice and mercy. Though revolting to the Jew, crucifixion remained one of the most popular of Roman pastimes, and particularly in the war against the Jews."

Q.   How do you define Zionism?

A.   The belief that those Jews who want to live in Israel have a right to do so, and a subsequent willingness to help that endeavor.

Q.   In an Orthodox synagogue why are women and men separated?

A.   Because women distract men, and vice versa.

Q.   Does the word, Torah, mean law?

A.   Not exactly. It means "instruction", and is more closely related to the classroom than the courtroom.

Q.   What is Midrash?

A.   Derived from a Hebrew word meaning "to dig," Midrash is that portion of the commentaries on the

Bible seeking to explore Holy Writ for lessons suitable to contemporary times. A cognate word, often used in Yiddish, is drush, meaning sermon.

Q. Does Judaism have sacraments?

A. No. The ceremonies (circumcision, marriage, etc.) in Judaism which resemble sacraments are designed to transport the individuals involved towards sanctification, not transform them.

Q. Explain Pidyon Ha-Ben.

A. Ben means son and ha means the. Pidyon means redemption of. According to the Bible, the first-born son of a Jewish mother belongs to the priesthood, but the parents could "redeem" him in a ceremony in which a descendant of the ancient priests would relinquish him.

Q. What does Oneg Shabbat mean?

A. The pleasure of the Sabbath. The Sabbath is traditionally designated as a time not only of rest and study but of joy. Hence during the Sabbath we should find time for edification, edibles, etc.

Q. What does the word, yahrzeit, mean?

A. It's German for the time (zeit) of the year (yahr), that is, the anniversary, of someone's demise.

Q. How old is Bar Mitzvah?

A. It was a "reform" introduced in the 12th century. Page 51 of this book begins a chapter devoted to a description of the origin of Bar Mitzvah.

Q. Is the Wailing Wall a term used by Jews?

A. Some do. But actually it is referred to in Israel as the Kotel (wall) Ha-maaravi (western).

Q. What does the word Hatikvah mean?

A. Tikvah means Hope. Ha means the.

Q. What does El Al mean?

A. El means to; Al (pronounced ahl) means on.

Q. Who introduced the Genocide resolution?

A. One of the finest men who ever lived, Dr. Raphael Lemkin, who lost 32 relatives to Nazism. He invented the word, genocide, and labored mightily to promulgate the resolution against genocide for the consideration of the UN. Many nations have ratified the resolution, but not the United States. For shame! Many men have been honored by the UN, but not Lemkin, who died some years ago. For shame!

Q. What is Sephardic Hebrew?

A. Sepharad (Tzefarad, actually) is a Hebrew word for Spain. Sephardic Jews are those Jews who lived in Spain, Northern Africa and Southern Europe. Their Hebrew pronunciation is different from that of the Ashkenazic Jews (Ashkenaz, orignally Germany, is a term applied to the Jews of Northern Europe). When Israel introduced modern Hebrew as its national parlance, it adopted the Sephardic type of pronunciation, and many synagogues have followed suit in their worship services. The chief differences between Ashkenazic and Sephardic Hebrew is that the former's aw becomes an ah, some of the former's s sounds are rendered like a t, and the Ashkenazi o becomes something like an uh.

Q.   Who said, What does the Lord require of thee? Only to do justly, love mercy, and walk humbly with thy God?

A.   The prophet, Micah. See Chapter 6, verse 8.

Q.   Is the name, Jonathan, Hebrew?

A.   Yes. It means "God gave."

Q.   What is the Jewish attitude towards Jesus?

A.   He is regarded as a great teacher, but not divine.

Q.   What is the Jewish view of the Messiah?

A.   There is no one Jewish view. Indeed, the Jewish Bible says less about the Messiah than is frequently supposed. The word, messiah, is Hebrew for "one who has oil placed on his head," i.e., a king. When the Jews were oppressed, they longed for a deliverer, but there was no unanimity about his nature. Some traditionalist Jews still look forward to a personal messiah; others believe that man can produce a messianic age.

Q.   Is Israel a theocracy?

A.   No. In a theocracy, the head of the government is also the religious leader. Such is not the case in Israel.

Q.   Where are the Ten Commandments to be found?

A.   They appear twice in the Jewish Bible: once in the 20th chapter of the Book of Exodus, and again in the 5th chapter of the Book of Deuteronomy (with some variations in language).

Q. What is Kosher?

A. It's a Hebrew word meaning proper, and refers to those foods which are prepared in accordance with traditional rules, or are not banned in Scriptures.

Q. What is the Talmud?

A. The Talmud is a vast corpus of literature which forms a commentary on a commentary of the Bible. The first layer of commentary is called the Mishnah (Reiteration). The second is called the Gemara (Conclusion). Both form the Talmud, a collection of interpretations and sermons based on Scriptures.

Q. What is Mazal Tov?

A. Literally the term means Good Star, and is the Hebrew expression for "Congratulations."

Q. What does L'Shanah Tovah mean?

A. Literally, "For a Good Year," but it is the way Jews wish each other "A Happy New Year."

Q. Is Yiddish a form of Hebrew?

A. No. Yiddish is a most reputable language written in Hebrew letters but derived from German, with many loans from other languages, and with a library of its own, idioms, and an enormous literature.

Q. Do Jews believe in an after-life?

A. Some do; others don't. In the Bible, there are few references to a hereafter. Later, Judaism borrowed some notions about some form of existence after death. But the doctrine never was fully accepted by all Jews. Some, of course, believe in personal immortality; others hope that there is some kind of continuation of the spirit or soul of every individual.

Q. What are the three Jewish denominations?

A. Orthodoxy, a clinging to past practices; Reform, which clings to traditional ideals but is hospitable to changes in practices; and Conservatism, which is somewhere between the other two groups.

INDEX

DATE DUE			
MAY 2 9 1986			